When Illness Becomes The Teacher

Jennifer Terry Martin

Dedication

To my husband Todd, my partner and safe place—thank you for
walking beside me through every season and loving me
with a steady, sacred kind of devotion—and for the laughter that
has carried us through it all.

Contents

Preface

This book has been a turning point in my journey. Writing it has asked me to trust that my voice has value, that the struggles and lessons I've carried might offer something to someone else. It has invited me to believe that the parts I once hid could become a bridge to connection. Each page has been a small act of surrender—setting aside control, letting the truth unfold, allowing the words to take shape. Over the years of walking a path of mindfulness and healing, something in me has softened, and this book weaves that way of being—paying attention, meeting life as it is—through my story. I've learned that hiding tightens the grip of shame, while honesty—first with myself, then with others—loosens it and opens the door to healing. Writing this book has been its own unfolding—one I could never have scripted. As the words took shape, my life opened in ways I never expected but always hoped were possible.

What I learned in those days of uncertainty isn't limited to life with Multiple Sclerosis. We all encounter seasons when the ground gives way—when life changes without our permission. It may arrive through illness, loss, the end of a relationship, the death of someone we love, or the quiet grief of a life not unfolding as we hoped. The circumstances vary, but the invitation remains the same: to loosen our grip on what we thought should be and learn to rest in what is.

For me, that invitation arrived with a diagnosis of MS and in its own way, through my writing. Putting words to the page became my private practice of honesty, and living with MS made that practice real. It showed me that the raw, vulnerable parts I once feared were not flaws to conceal or fix but pathways to courage, connection, and healing. And maybe that is why, after all these years of silencing myself and hiding my deepest parts, I was finally ready to write this book. It is my testimony to the healing power that arises when we dare to look within and allow ourselves to be seen.

PROLOGUE

I stood in the shower beneath a stream of warm water, the neurologist's words echoing in my mind. *"You most likely have Multiple Sclerosis. It's okay to be upset—this is devastating news. You will likely be in a wheelchair one day."* The future I had imagined—one where I was strong, capable, in control—felt like it was slipping through my fingers.

Everything should have felt like it was shattering. But instead of panic, a deep steady calm settled over me. It was quiet, unmistakable, and almost impossible to explain. It was as if something beyond me whispered: *This is not happening to you. This is happening for you.*

I didn't know what lay ahead—the uncertainty, the challenges, the moments that would test me in ways I could not yet fathom. But in that moment, I felt one clear truth: *I was not alone and I was okay.*

Looking back now, more than twenty years later, I recognize that moment for what it was. That peace was *grace*. For me, that was God.

Fear could have swallowed me whole. But instead, I was given something else—*an inner knowing that this journey, as difficult as it might be, would also be a teacher.*

Overtime, MS has come to stand for much more than Multiple Sclerosis. It has come to mean **MySelf**. This illness—this unwelcome, unpredictable companion—became one of my greatest teachers. It slowed me down. It asked me to listen. It revealed strength I didn't know I had. It showed me how joy can coexist alongside uncertainty.

And now, the same quiet voice that met me in the weight of that impossible news is asking me to share my story.

Whether you are living with a chronic illness, supporting someone who is, or simply finding your way through life's unexpected turns, my hope is that something within these pages reminds you:

You are not alone.

There is wisdom in the hardship.

There is softness in the breaking.

There is light always waiting to be found.

Part One:
When Life Changed Overnight

1

THE CHRISTMAS THAT CHANGED EVERYTHING

"We cannot choose to vanish the dark, but we can choose to spark a light." — Dr. Edith Eger

The twinkling lights on the Christmas tree cast a warm glow across the living room, their soft flicker reflected in the glass ornaments placed carefully days earlier by our daughters, Carly and Lindsey. Laughter from our Christmas Eve gathering still lingered in the air, the scent of cinnamon and pine filling the house. But beneath it all, a dull, insistent throb pulsed at my temples. I blinked hard, willing it away. There was no time to be anything but *fine.*

Snow blanketed the streets outside—a classic New England Christmas Eve. Inside, Todd and I stayed up long past bedtime, acquiescing to that familiar pressure to make everything magical for Carly and Lindsey. He wrestled with a bicycle and an art easel while I sat curled over the kitchen table, eyes tired, hand cramping, carefully shaping each letter of Santa's reply. It was the fourth year I'd copied the same elaborate, scroll-heavy handwriting I'd foolishly committed to on Carly's first Christmas. Every year I swore I'd simplify. And every year, I didn't. There was something sacred in the ritual—each squiggle a silent vow to preserve their wonder just a little longer. Looking back, it's amazing they never questioned why the Easter Bunny and Tooth Fairy wrote exactly like Santa...but with more glitter.

Exhaustion pressed down on me. My head throbbed—a dull, relentless ache that had lingered for days. A quiet, buzzing tension pulsed beneath my skin—too faint to explain, too present to dismiss. I couldn't name it, but I could feel it. But there were presents to wrap, food to prepare, tables to set, and two little girls fast asleep, dreaming of Christmas morning. So, I ignored it, convincing myself I was overtired. Nothing more.

I bent down to pick up a stray ribbon from the floor and wobbled, a wave of disorientation washing over me. Strange. I steadied myself, brushing off the brief spell of dizziness. Just fatigue, I told myself. "I need sleep," I muttered, half to myself, half to Todd, who was adjusting the handlebars on Carly's new bike. The window caught my reflection - subtle but unmistakable: pale skin, tired eyes, and a tension in my face I didn't recognize. I pressed my fingers to my temples, trying to dismiss the unease.

By the time we finally collapsed into bed, Santa had left his mark—cookie crumbs scattered on the plate, a half-empty glass of milk, and the shimmer of glittered oatmeal dusting the lawn. I paused, taking it in. The magic of childhood, so fleeting yet so vivid in this moment. I wanted to freeze time, to memorize every last detail. But as I lay down, the ache in my head pulsed harder, a dull, rhythmic pounding. A whisper of unease curled in my stomach. Something wasn't right. I felt it. I rolled over, exhaling. It's just exhaustion. Tomorrow, I'll be fine.

Christmas Day was a blur of wrapping paper and laughter, family and festive culinary delights filling every corner of the house.

The warmth and chaos felt familiar, comforting. If I was exhaust-ed, it was due to the whirlwind of hosting two holiday gatherings back-to-back. That's what I told myself, anyway. But by evening, as I scooped up a stray toy, a sharp pulse of pain shot through my skull. The headache, relentless and unmoving, had not faded. If anything, it was digging in deeper. And it wasn't alone. Something else was creeping in - a pressure, a weight, a quiet knowing. This was not exhaustion.

The next morning, we piled into the car for some post-holiday errands, the girls buckled into their car seats, chattering about their new toys. But as Todd pulled out of the driveway, I felt it—an unfamiliar ache deep in my eye sockets. Every time I moved my eyes, pain stabbed through them, sharp and insistent. I winced and rubbed my temples. "This is weird. My eyes hurt when I move them." Todd glanced over, unconcerned. "Sounds like an ocular migraine. I get them all the time." Relief washed over me. That had to be it. A migraine. Something ordinary. Nothing to worry about.

As the day wore on, my vision blurred at the edges. Words on signs, once crisp, began to smear together. I blinked hard, trying to refocus, but the world stayed slightly out of reach. Later that afternoon, as I moved through the grocery store, I reached for a cereal box and traced the edge with my fingers, willing the letters to come into focus. They didn't. I looked up at the aisle sign - more fuzz. The words bled together, shapeless and unreadable. My heart kicked. I turned to one label after another. Nothing made sense. My breath hitched as a sharp prickle of fear crept up my spine. Carly tugged at my sleeve. "Mommy, can I get the animal crackers?" Her voice felt far away. I nodded, barely processing, my hand tightening around the cart for balance. Something was wrong. Deeply wrong.

It was a holiday weekend—no doctor's office open, no easy answers. I drove to a nearby urgent care, clinging to the hope someone would have an explanation that made sense. The doctor barely looked at me before giving his verdict. "Sinus infection," he asserted. "Pressure behind the eyes can cause vision issues. Just take some Sudafed, and you should be fine." I nodded numbly, but as I walked out the door, I already knew I would not be stopping at the pharmacy for Sudafed. I wasn't losing my eyesight because of a sinus infection. I didn't even have a stuffy nose. Left with no answers, a growing sense of unease settled in my chest.

That night, after tucking the girls into bed, I sat on the edge of my own bed, blinking into the darkness. My field of vision was shrinking. I could feel the edges of my world closing in. Fear coiled in my chest. Was I having a stroke? I called the emergency room, my fingers trembling as I pressed the buttons. I clutched the phone to my ear, the dial tone stretching too long before a nurse's voice broke through. I tried to keep my voice steady. "My vision is going. It's getting worse. Do I need to come in?" Her response was calm, too calm. "We don't have the equipment to assess that," she said, her tone efficient, detached. My fingers tightened around the receiver. "But my vision is getting worse," I pressed. Silence. Then, "You'll need to see an ophthalmologist."

That was it. No urgency, no directive to come in. I hung up and stared at the ceiling in the dark. My breath was shallow, my mind racing. I considered waking Todd. I thought about going to the ER anyway. Instead, I pulled the covers tighter around me, closed my eyes, and begged morning to come. I hoped and prayed that by morning I'd open my eyes and everything would be normal again.

When I woke up the next morning, something felt different. My left eye—was it slightly better? I blinked a few times, hesitant hope flickering. But as I tried to take in the room around me, a terrible realization hit. The vision in my right eye wasn't just blurry—it was nearly gone! Only a hazy, muted world remained, as if a thick fog had descended over everything. Panic prickled up my spine. I blinked harder, turned my head, tried to focus. Nothing changed. Half my vision was slipping away, and I couldn't stop it.

It was now Sunday of the holiday weekend—still no doctors, still no answers. The unease in my chest escalated into full-blown dread. Then I remembered our neighbor was an ophthalmologist. Gripping my phone, I left him a message, my voice steadier than I felt. Hours later, he called back. He was out of town but promised to open his office first thing in the morning. I exhaled. One more night and I would have some answers.

"Look straight ahead," my neighbor instructed, adjusting the slit lamp as I pressed my chin into the holder. The light seared into my eye, too bright, too sharp. My pulse thrummed in my ears. He frowned, shifting the lens. A pause. Then, a slow exhale. "You have a severe case of optic neuritis." The words landed like a kick in the gut. My fingers curled into my lap, "What does that mean?" My voice was too steady, as if saying it calmly might make it less true. He met my gaze. "It means we need to find out what's causing it." And just like that, the ground beneath me tilted. His voice was calm, but the words carried weight. He explained that optic neuritis is an inflammation of the second cranial nerve, and while the cause was still unknown, it wasn't something to ignore.

What followed was a blur of medical urgency—he sent me for an immediate CT scan to rule out a blood clot. When that came back clear, I was referred to a neurologist for further testing. The possibilities hung in the air like a menacing storm cloud: a brain tumor, lupus, MS. I barely had time to process any of it before the neurologist started me on a round of high-dose IV steroids, hoping to reduce the inflammation and restore at least some of my vision. It seemed to be happening too fast and too slow at the same time. I wasn't ready for any part of this—but I had no choice.

Since this occurred before the advanced technology available today, it meant waiting weeks, not days, for real answers. And in those weeks, I did what I had always done when faced with uncertainty: I pushed my fear down and buried it beneath the rhythm of daily life. I poured all of my energy into taking care of our daughters, who were just 4 ½ and almost 2 at the time. If I stayed busy enough, maybe I wouldn't have to think about what was happening. I was 35, healthy—this couldn't be something serious. It had to be something explainable, temporary. And so, I clung to the safest explanation I could dredge up: my first-ever flu shot a month earlier. That had to be it. It was easier to believe this than face the growing fear of a bigger problem unfolding.

The fragile hope that all of this was just a reaction to the flu shot shattered the moment I stepped into the neurologist's office and saw my MRI scans illuminated on the light box. He slid one into place and paused. White streaks lit up the image—bright and unmistakable against the gray matter of my brain.

His voice became distant, almost mechanical, like the muffled, garbled voice of the teacher in a Charlie Brown episode. "The lesions on your brain are indicative of Multiple Sclerosis." He didn't soften the blow. No buildup. No cushion. The words hit like a kick in the gut - sudden, blunt, irreversible. I froze, my mind scrambling to keep up. It felt like being handed someone else's life mid-sentence.

The diagnosis settled in—uninvited, but determined to stay. My breath stilled. My heartbeat thundered in my ears. Did he really just say that? A tightness gripped my ribs and my breath turned shallow, the air in the room suddenly too thin. A silence stretched between us, thick and suffocating. The roaring in my ears was sure to drown out whatever he'd say next. Todd's hand was on my knee, solid and warm, but I couldn't turn to meet his gaze. The room, the words, the reality—I could not hold it all at once.

Fighting back tears, I whispered, "I need a moment," gripping the edge of the chair, trying to steady myself. My body already knew this was life-changing, even if my mind hadn't caught up yet. Then, with the same detached tone, the neurologist added, "It's okay to cry—this is devastating news. You will likely be in a wheelchair one day." His words sliced through the air, cold and absolute. Did he really just map out my future with such certainty—such *cruelty*? A surge of anger rose beneath the shock, hot and unrelenting.

Something surged in me - sharp, electric, undeniable. A flicker of defiance rising through the numbness. I refused to accept his prophecy as truth. My hands trembled as I grabbed my MRI films, stood up, and walked out. In the elevator, the fluorescent lights felt too bright. I pressed my fingers against my temples to steady myself, his words reverberating in my head. *Devastating. Wheelchair.* I could see Todd watching me, waiting for something—anger, fear, collapse. Instead, I straightened, inhaled, and steadied my voice.

"We are finding a new neurologist," I stated, the steel in my tone surprising even me. Todd nodded, squeezing my hand. And that was that. For now.

Pause and Reflect

• Think of a time when you dismissed your body's signals. What might have happened if you had paused and listened? Can you forgive yourself for not having done so?

• How do you typically react to uncertainty? Do you try to control the situation, avoid it, or push through?

• What small moments of presence - like the Christmas magic - do you cherish in your life? How can you savor them more?

2

THE MOMENT OF AWAKENING

"Awakening is not a process of building ourselves up but a process of letting go." — Pema Chödrön

I watched Todd's knuckles turn white against the steering wheel, his gaze fixed straight ahead. I wanted to tell him we would be okay, that we would figure this out together. But how could I when I had no idea what was coming? The words sat heavy in my chest, lodged somewhere between my heart and throat. So, I stayed silent.

Todd reached over, his fingers curling around mine. "It'll be okay, Wookie." Wookie. The pet- name we gave each other years before. A word that usually made me smile, but tonight, it merely hung in the space between us. I don't think he knew what else to say. We were both still processing. His voice was gentle, but I could hear the uncertainty beneath it. We were grasping for reassurance, trying to steady ourselves in the unknown. I squeezed his hand in return, finding an odd comfort in the silence where words felt useless. Maybe it was because, despite everything, some small part of me was starting to stir, whispering that we would find our way.

The oncoming traffic blurred through my tears as my thoughts spiraled. What if I can't chase our daughters in the yard? What if I am not the mother they need? What if I am a burden? I pressed my forehead against the cool glass of the passenger window and whispered my plea: *God, just let me be okay until they go off to college. Then I will accept whatever comes next.*

The moment I walked into the house, I straightened my shoulders, forcing normalcy into my body. Todd looked at me, searching my face for something—maybe fear, maybe truth, but I gave him neither. Instead, I smiled—too bright, too steady—performer sticking to the script. "It's going to be okay," I said, my voice lighter than I felt, as if saying it with enough conviction might make it true.

Carly and Lindsey came running, arms outstretched. "Mommy!" Their little hands clung to me as I scooped them up, their tiny arms wrapping around my neck with the kind of unbridled joy only children have. Their giggles and warmth wrapped me in a blanket of love, a momentary illusion that everything was okay. I closed my eyes. I wanted to freeze this feeling and let their embrace anchor me in something familiar. "Mommy's home," I whispered. But was I? I felt like a ghost in my own body, present but untethered, as if I were sleepwalking through a life I could barely recognize.

Over the next few days, I answered messages from family and friends with the same automatic response: "I'm okay. Everything is fine." But nothing felt fine. I was unraveling in silence, too afraid to let anyone see how terrified I was.

This need to present a brave, confident front wasn't new to me, but this moment felt like uncharted terrain. I had been raised with the belief that positivity was a form of strength, that composure matters, and that appearances carry weight. Even as fear churned inside me, I felt that old, familiar pressure to appear strong, to be unwavering, to convince everyone—my family, my friends, and myself that I was fine.

My mother had always been a worrier. She lost her sister in her thirties, and I imagine that loss left her carrying a fear she never fully put down. As a result, I took on an unspoken role: the one who reassured, who steadied, who didn't add to her worries. Over time, I learned to perform—to protect. I overcompensated. I smiled a little brighter and spoke with a little more certainty, all in an effort to keep everyone else calm. But beneath my mask, the pressure was mounting. In trying to shield others from my fear, I unknowingly locked myself out of feeling it too.

At night, sleep became a battle. My body begged for rest, but my mind refused to comply. Night after night, I tossed and turned, trying to will away the fear clawing at my chest. When I finally drifted off, it never lasted long. I would jolt awake to a sudden rush in my head, a wave of lightheadedness that rolled through me, leaving me unsteady and shaken even while lying still. My body would begin to shake, as if a surge of adrenaline had been released all at once, flooding my system without warning. The disorientation was immediate and terrifying. Each time, I braced myself for the worst. Was I about to faint? Was this a heart attack? Was I dying?

Over time, I learned to reason with the panic. *You've felt this before. You're okay.* Some nights, I almost believed it. Other nights, the doubt was insurmountable. I would bolt out of bed, my breath erratic and my legs shaky beneath me, and make my way to the kitchen. Standing in the dark, bare feet pressing into the cool tile, my fingers traced absentminded circles along the granite counter-top.

The hum of the refrigerator filled the silence, steady and unchanging, as if the world itself had not tilted beneath me. The faint glow on the microwave clock cast elongated shadows across the room, its green numbers blurring as I squinted and willed them into focus. I reached for a glass, the smooth weight of it grounding me for a moment before I filled it with water, listening to the quiet rush as it poured. I took small sips, letting the cold liquid slide down my throat, focusing on the simple act of swallowing.

The coolness spread through me, cutting through the wave of panic. It was like turning down the volume on a blaring radio — suddenly, there was space to think. Somehow, the sensation of drinking, the movement of my throat, the crisp contrast between my burning anxiety and the cool water, began to steady me. I was searching for something I could not yet name — only that the feel of the glass in my hand and the simple rhythm of swallowing anchored me long enough for the fear to pass.

A cracker, dry and bland, crumbled between my fingers as I nibbled at the edges — more out of habit than hunger. Anything to ground myself. Anything to convince my body I was safe. And slowly, I was. The worst of the fear receded. Not entirely. Not permanently. But enough. Enough to exhale, to loosen my grip, to take one more sip. When I finally returned to bed, relief washed over me — paired with a quiet gratitude that it had passed, and the lingering fear of when it might return. By morning, the panic had loosened its grip, but it hadn't left me entirely. It lingered beneath the surface, a low hum of unease I carried with me into the day.

I remember one afternoon when the unease began to rise again, and I needed to be alone, so I escaped to the shower. The water hit my shoulders, hot and steady, but I barely felt it. I tilted my head back, letting the steam rise around me. My body was there, standing beneath the spray, but my mind was still running—spinning, unraveling, reaching for answers that didn't exist. *Maybe I need to cry.* The thought flickered across my mind, a quiet permission I had not yet granted myself. But another part of me resisted. *What if I let go and can't stop? What if I fall apart?* I could still hear the echoes of expectation—internalized voices shaped by childhood lessons, urging me to be strong, to be brave, to hold my shit together.

But as the steam thickened and the water traced warm paths down my skin, something shifted.   My breath steadied. The pounding in my head softened. The panic loosened its grip, enough for me to notice a difference. And then, in the stillness, something else emerged—not a voice but a knowing, deep and certain. *This is not happening to you. It is happening for you.*

I blinked, my breath steady now. The water still poured over me, but suddenly, I felt it. Every drop. Every sensation. The weight in my chest lifted, just slightly, just enough. I had no answers, but for the first time since hearing the words *Multiple Sclerosis*, I had peace.

I wrapped myself in a towel, steam curling around me, and caught my reflection in the fogged-up mirror. My face looked the same, yet something in my eyes had shifted—something softer, quieter. The fear wasn't gone, but it no longer owned me. I pressed my palms against my chest, feeling the quiet rhythm of my breath. Whatever came next, I wasn't meeting it alone. There was a presence with me—quiet, steady, and unmistakable. It felt like something larger was holding me, even if I couldn't quite name it.

I didn't know what this sense of peace meant or how long it would last. I only knew something had shifted—and maybe, just maybe, I didn't have to fight this as hard as I thought. I couldn't yet see that this marked the beginning of a slow, steady awakening. What I was beginning to learn—without realizing it—was how to stay with my experience rather than brace against it. That MS, the very thing I feared, would bring to light parts of myself—quiet, hidden places I might otherwise have missed. It would become one of my greatest teachers.

I didn't yet realize that losing my eyesight would, in many ways, help me see more clearly than ever before. At the time, MS felt like something was being taken from me. I could not yet see that this illness would eventually reveal its gifts.

In the years that followed, I came to understand that it was also giving me something—an invitation to grow, to heal, to live with greater awareness. What once felt like an unwelcome intruder would, in time, reveal itself as a guide - a force that would push me to pay attention, to listen, to trust myself in ways I never did before. MS would come to stand for MySelf: teaching me, again and again, who I was and what I was capable of becoming.

Pause and Reflect

- When in your life have you felt the pressure to put on a brave face or be "fine" for others, even when you were struggling?

- Have you ever had a moment of unexpected peace in the midst of chaos? Where do you think it came from? What did it feel like?

- If you could look back at a difficult moment with fresh eyes, what do you think it was trying to teach you? Did you realize it before now? How has it helped or benefitted you in your life?

- If the lesson just came to you in an "aha" moment, how might you apply it to your life?

3

FINDING MY PATH THROUGH ANXIETY AND FEAR

"Perhaps the biggest tragedy of our lives is that freedom is possible, yet we can pass our years trapped in the same old patterns... The good news is that you can open to truth, love, and freedom right now." —
Tara Brach

One morning, I woke up to sunlight streaming through the window. For a moment, I stretched, listening to the quiet hum of the house. Had I dreamt it all—the blur, the fear, the doctor's words? Maybe I could slip back into life...before.

I tiptoed downstairs, craving the quiet before the day began. These early mornings were always mine: a warm mug of tea in my hands, the world still hushed and waiting. In those moments, before the weight of the day settled in, I could almost convince myself nothing had changed.

But as I lifted my cup to take a sip, reality came rushing back. The illusion shattered. My vision was still blurred - a lens smudged with fingerprints I couldn't wipe away. I blinked harder, but the familiar fog remained. While I was grateful to have sight in my left eye, the vision in my right felt like I had taken both hands and pressed in from either side, shrinking my field of vision to a pinprick. With both eyes open, the world looked whole, but when I covered my left eye, all I could see was a single dot of light surrounded by thick, hazy darkness. My vision had not yet improved as I'd so desperately hoped. And just like that, the fear returned.

Desperate for reassurance, I began testing my vision constantly. Every time I entered the kitchen, my eyes darted to the microwave clock. If I could just make out the glowing numbers, maybe I could believe this wasn't happening. Maybe it was getting better. But each time, the digits blurred, swimming just out of reach. My stomach dropped. My heart raced. It became a ritual, a hidden obsession, a battle with a reality I wasn't ready to accept. And with each failed attempt, the panic tightened its grip.

That same day, curled up with my daughters, I was given a rare and precious glimpse of normalcy. Carly and Lindsey nestled against me, their warm bodies pressed against my sides, tiny fingers flipping pages with eager delight. Their giggles rose like bubbles through the quiet room, and for a moment I was not the woman bracing for the next symptom. I was not a body under siege. I was Mommy—safe—whole, and wrapping my daughters in the comfort of story and laughter. Instinctively, I closed my left eye. A quick test. A flicker of hope. But without the help of my stronger eye, the words on the page wavered and dissolved. My chest seized, the air suddenly sharp. The moment unraveled, stripping my sense of safety and pulling me back into the dreaded grip of fear. The ground beneath me gave way once more—and I was falling.

It was a moment I wouldn't fully understand until much later: how swiftly peace can disappear and fear reclaim the space. But that moment also planted a question, a possibility. If calm could vanish in a breath, perhaps it could return just as quickly. Mindfulness would later give language to a quiet truth: every moment holds the potential for beginning again. But I wasn't there yet. Not even close.

I forced a brave face for everyone else, determined not to let my fear become their burden. I had learned how to reassure, how to steady the room. I could still hold my daughters close, still read to them and smile when I needed to. "I'm fine," I'd say, even as my chest tightened and my thoughts spiraled. But the truth was, inside, I was becoming unhinged. And without warning, the panic attacks began to intensify.

There was no real pattern, no trigger I could predict. Panic didn't announce itself—it arrived like a switch flipping inside me: a sudden rush of heat, the quickening of my pulse, a tightening in my chest.

One moment I'd be fine, and the next my body would turn on me—tingling, dizzy, like I might pass out, and with it came a wave of fear I couldn't outrun. One winter morning, I was standing in line at the bagel shop. The scent of warm bread filled the air, mixing with the sharper notes of coffee and toasted sesame. Carly's small hand was tucked in mine, her chatter rising and falling beneath the hum of the room. Around us, the shop bustled with activity—mothers wrestling with strollers, toddlers squealing, conversations stacking on top of each other.

The overhead lights buzzed, casting a harsh, sterile glow. I noticed the cold too—the way the door's draft crept in, numbing my fingers even through my gloves. Everything around me was loud. Bright. Too much. And then, that strange sensation again— like I was watching the scene from somewhere just behind me. My body was there, but I wasn't in it. My thoughts scattered, untethered. The harder I tried to pull myself back, the farther away I drifted. All I could feel was the overwhelm rising. The world was happening around me, and I was slipping out of it.

Instantly, an invisible fist closed around my ribs. My breath caught. The hum of happy voices turned to static. The steady lights above began to pulse, flickering in time with my racing heart. My vision narrowed at the edges and colors dulled. My hands tingled and my knees wobbled.

"You're fine," I told myself. "Just breathe." But nothing felt fine. The noise in the shop dulled, as if someone had turned the volume down on the world. The air grew dense, pressing against my chest, each breath shallow as the room closed in and shrunk around me.

Carly's fingers tugged mine, grounding me—but even her small presence felt far away, like I was underwater. The room tilted and a wave of nausea surged. I needed to leave, but my legs were locked in place. I reached for the counter—not to place an order, but to hold on. The smooth, chilled surface pressed back against my fingertips. It was the only thing that felt real—solid, unmoving, indifferent to the chaos inside me. I tried to anchor myself to it, as if its stillness could steady the storm inside me. "Hold on," I whispered. "Just hold on."

No one else in the shop noticed. The world kept moving. Questions rushed at me from every corner of my brain. *Why is my body shutting down? Should I call for help?* I needed to get outside. *What if I faint on the sidewalk? Will the girls be alright?* My heart was racing too fast. This wasn't normal. This wasn't okay.

By the time the episode passed, I was exhausted—shaking, like my body had been holding something heavy for too long. I didn't know it then, but I had been trying to stay with my experience rather than run from it. Carly tugged at my hand, eager for her bagel, while I tried to recover from the fear storm that had swept through my body. And then came the unexpected part: the fear didn't leave. It morphed into anticipation. *What if this happens again?*

The next morning, I considered going back to the bagel shop, but my hands tingled just thinking about it. Even imagining it made my stomach turn. *What if the panic returns the moment I step inside?* So, I decided against it. Soon I started avoiding other places as well—crowded stores, parking lots, anywhere I might feel exposed or too far from help. My world was shrinking fast, and I had no idea how to stop it. At the time, I had no idea my senses could become allies. I didn't yet know how to work with mindfulness as a tool—how to use the warmth of Carly's hand, the rhythm of my own breath, the feeling of the floor beneath me as anchors. Back then, these were mere details in the blur. Later, they became the very things that carried me through.

Soon, the panic followed me into the car. I would be driving on the highway, and suddenly I'd be dizzy, my chest tightening and pulse racing. The sensations sent a jolt of fear through me each time, convincing me I needed to get off the road immediately. It felt safer to avoid the highways altogether. So, I did. I stopped taking I-95 and the Merritt Parkway, choosing the long way around to avoid the on-ramps. But the more I avoided, the worse it got. The dread wasn't diminishing; it was intensifying—tightening its relentless strangle hold on me.

What if I start to fear driving altogether? The thought terrified me more than the panic attacks. I was a mother of two young children. I couldn't let fear shrink my world—not when two little girls were counting on me to move them through their lives. But how was I supposed to stop something that felt bigger and more powerful than me?

I had to take action. I needed answers—not only for my vision, the panic attacks, and the spiraling fears, but for all of it. If I could understand what was happening in my body, maybe I could find a way to regain control. And so, I did what I've always done when faced with uncertainty—I researched. I threw myself into learning everything I could about MS, desperate to understand what I was up against. One concept kept surfacing—stress matters. Over and over, I read that stress could trigger relapses and make symptoms worse. It became clear: if I wanted to have any control over my health, I needed to learn how to manage my stress.

But this realization only made things worse. I felt trapped in a cycle of being stressed about being stressed, and I knew avoiding it wasn't an option. Maybe I could learn to meet it differently. I didn't know how yet, but I was determined to find out. As fate would have it, I came across a book that would change everything—*Full Catastrophe Living* by Jon Kabat-Zinn. His work at the University of Massachusetts offered something radical and deeply hopeful: evidence that mindfulness can actually rewire the brain. That it can change how we relate to stress; not by avoiding it, but by approaching it another way.

For the first time, I felt a sense of relief. Kabat-Zinn's eight-week Mindfulness-Based Stress Reduction course was being used with patients facing cancer, heart conditions, chronic pain, and other stress-related illnesses. These patients weren't changing their diagnoses; they were learning to relate to them differently.

I couldn't change the fact that I had MS, but I could change how I lived with it—how I met it, moment by moment. This wasn't abstract theory—there was science behind what I was reading. It wasn't vague advice or wishful thinking; it was information grounded in research and backed by results. I had been hoping for something like this. Something to help address my fear and my need to understand my body. Something that didn't ask me to be perfect—just present.

As I read Kabat-Zinn's book, an unexpected feeling surfaced—hope. For the first time in months, I felt a sense of empowerment. There were tools I could learn, practices I could embrace—ways to meet the fear rather than be consumed by it. And I wasn't alone. Others were walking this same uncertain path, searching for peace, for ease, for a way to loosen the clutches of fear. Their stories reflected pieces of mine, and in them, I felt seen.

One idea rose above all—simple but profound: I couldn't control what was happening in my life, but I could choose how to respond. That impacted me. After months of helplessness, a small, steady glimmer of agency returned. I wasn't entirely at the mercy of my circumstances. I couldn't change the fact that MS was now a part of my life, but I could change the way I thought about it, responded to it, and how I lived with it and with myself. That one realization, that simple possibility, felt like a beacon of light breaking through after a long, dark night.

Not long after finishing *Full Catastrophe Living*, life handed me an opportunity too perfectly timed to ignore. A yoga teacher, one I deeply trusted and who had supported me through those first difficult months, announced she had gotten certified to teach the MBSR course—the very program I had been reading about. I could hardly believe it. I had been wondering how I might access this program, knowing a trip to Massachusetts with two small children was out of the question. And now, here it was—right in my own community—falling into my lap.

I wasn't someone who typically looked for signs, but this one was undeniable. I signed up for the eight-week course without hesitation, overwhelmed with gratitude—certain I was meant to be there. To say it changed my life would be an understatement. The course was simple in structure but challenging in practice: learning to sit, to pay attention, to notice what was happening in my body and mind—with curiosity rather than judgment.

At first, I wasn't sure I could sit still and pay attention to my breath. It seemed almost too simple, yet there I was, fidgeting, my thoughts racing. I sat cross-legged on the floor, unsure of myself. *Am I doing this right?* "Breathe," the instructor encouraged. "Notice the inhale, the exhale. Nothing to fix, just notice." Still, my mind refused to slow down. My body shifted uncomfortably, resisting the stillness. *This isn't working, I should be doing something.* But then, for a single breath, something loosened. I noticed the coolness at the tip of my nose. The way the air expanded my ribs. It was barely a flicker, but it was there. For the first time in weeks, I felt a moment of peace.

Slowly, I began to recognize the power of feeling anchored. Sometimes all it took was a few deep breaths, the sensation of my feet on the floor, or even a simple sip of water. I realized I had already been reaching for small tools long before I fully understood what I was doing. Carrying water with me—something I had begun doing without much thought—became my safety net; a silent reassurance that I had something to turn to when the fear snuck in. It wasn't about the water itself, but the knowing. The act of taking a sip reminded me I could do something—I wasn't entirely at the mercy of my panic. Those small moments of grounding began to stitch together a fragile sense of trust in myself. It gave me a foundation I could build on.

As the eight weeks drew to a close, I recognized that the new mindfulness techniques I was learning were not yet second nature. The foundation had been laid but without guidance and consistent practice, I was still on shaky ground. Without the structure of the course, I feared slipping back into old patterns and losing the foothold I had only just begun to gain.

And then, out of the blue, my teacher pulled me aside and asked if I'd be willing to assist her in the next course. In exchange, I could take it again—this time as both a participant and support person. I said yes without hesitation. The universe was giving me a gentle nudge to stay the course. What a gift.

Each week, I arrived early to help set up the class in the church basement—easels, chairs, notepads, pens. It became peaceful ritual, one that kept me close to the practices I was still learning to trust. Working as an assistant not only gave me another eight weeks to deepen my practice, it also allowed me to witness other students moving through the course. I saw them experiencing the same shifts and knew I was not alone.

One week, I wasn't feeling well at all. My nervous system felt frayed for no apparent reason, and I debated whether I should go. Knowing the teacher was counting on me, I pushed through the discomfort. This was early in my journey with MS, before I fully understood the importance of honoring my body's signals.

As I arranged the room that evening, a familiar wave of panic overtook me. I got dizzy, unsteady—like I might faint. Once everything for the class was in place, I approached the teacher and, with a shaky voice, tried to explain I was feeling off. I felt a pang of guilt, like I was letting her down by leaving, but another part of me knew *this was the practice.* Listening to my body. Meeting myself where I was. Trying to live what I was learning, even if it meant stepping away from doing something I cared about—and risking disappointing someone else in the process.

That moment became one of many where I'd need to step away from commitments—something I once saw as failure but later came to understand as self-respect. Over time, I learned to build buffers around important commitments and events. If I had to show up in a big way, I created space before and after—to rest, to recover, to breathe. It became an insurance policy for my well-being.

In the remaining weeks of the course, I took extra care on class days—moving slower, building in space, letting go of pressure. It was always needed. Making space to rest wasn't indulgent—it was necessary. And choosing it without guilt marked a new kind of strength.

Life outside the safety net of class remained complex. My health wasn't improving in the ways I had hoped, but slowly, the way I related to my body, to my fear, to my limits, began to change. And that changed everything. Over time, the panic attacks began to loosen their grip. I found myself checking the microwave clock less and less, and when I did, the blurry numbers no longer sent me spiraling. My vision wasn't improving, but it no longer felt like the most important thing.

Moment by moment, I was learning to be with life rather than brace against it. I began to savor the simple things in a new way—reading in bed with Carly and Lindsey, walking to the bus stop, feeling the sun on my skin. I started to see that so much of my anxiety wasn't rooted in my body. It was rooted in my thoughts. My mind raced ahead to prepare for what might go wrong: the what-ifs, the imagined futures, the pervasive fear I might not be able to cope. The biggest realization? *If I could stay in the present moment, I was okay. No matter what was happening—right here, right now—I was safe.*

The more I practiced, the faster I could recognize when my mind was drifting into the past or spinning into the future. And each time, it became a little bit easier to come back to the present moment. Back to now.

I used to cope by suppressing or ignoring. I'd shove my emotions down and keep them carefully hidden beneath the surface. The pressure to seem fine robbed me of being with what was really unfolding. When I was pretending to be okay, I had no way to sit with what was actually hard. It turns out I had to lose my sight in order to see. I was now learning to face things—to admit when things were hard and let them be as they were. It felt like I had been given a new way to be with my life. I wasn't changing my circumstances—I was changing the way I met them. Thirty minutes of meditation in the morning, a guided body scan before sleep—and over time, every part of my life began to shift.

The tight knot of stress I once carried began to loosen. I wasn't obsessing about every sensation or bracing for what might go wrong. I was learning to meet my moments with more patience, more breath, more presence. A steadiness began to grow within me. My days weren't suddenly easier. My challenges didn't disappear. But I had changed. And in that softening, a quiet trust in myself began to take root.

I stopped avoiding crowded places and busy highways. Fear didn't dictate my choices anymore. I trusted myself to meet it head on. When panic set in, I had my breath, my body, and mindfulness techniques to keep me anchored in the present moment. I could ground myself with deep, steady breaths. I could create space for compassion instead of bearing down with resistance. I could ease onto the highway, inhaling deeply as I merged, reminding myself: *I am safe.*

I still carried a water bottle—not just out of habit, but as a tangible reminder of the tools I had at my disposal. I wasn't powerless. Each time I met fear with steadiness instead of avoidance, my world expanded. I worried less. I enjoyed life more. And one day, I walked past the microwave without stopping to check the numbers.

Pause and Reflect

- Have you ever had an experience where fear began to control your life? How did you respond?

- What stress management tools do you currently use? How are they working for you?

- Think of a time when you thought you had "escaped" something difficult, only to have it resurface. How did you handle it?

- If you had to describe your relationship with uncertainty in one sentence, what would it be?

4

The News I Never Wanted to Hear

"Some changes look negative on the surface but you will soon realize that space is being created in your life for something new to emerge."
— Eckhart Tolle

For three years, my life hovered in uncertainty. My neurologist had warned me I likely had MS—an unpredictable autoimmune disease that affects the central nervous system and often unfolds in episodes over time—but certainty required my body to betray me again. All I could do was wait. Wait for another symptom, another flare, another signal from a body I could not control. I felt suspended and powerless, caught between what was suspected and what had yet to be proven.

At the time, I had experienced only a single episode of symptoms. A confirmed diagnosis required another—separated by time, affecting a different part of my body.

For three years, I did not have another episode of MS-like symptoms, so I told myself I was fine. Most days, I managed to believe it. I clung to the hope that the neurologist was wrong; that the optic neuritis was a one-time event, and that my body wasn't quietly turning against me. For a while, the story held, at least on the surface.

Beneath the surface was a steady effort on my part to hold things together. Not a show of strength exactly—more like survival dressed up as calm. I was a mother of two little girls, and life was busy. Between school drop-offs, birthday parties, and chaotic schedules, I didn't have time to sit around wondering if a neurological disease was lurking within. If I focused on the normalcy of life, I could forget, for a little while, that my body had already given me a warning sign. But in the quiet moments—when the house was still, the girls tucked safely in their beds, and my husband out of town—the doubt crept in. *What if the doctor wasn't wrong? What if this is the calm before the storm?*

At night, when everything finally went quiet, my body became impossible to ignore. Lying perfectly still in bed, I would try to detect the tiniest shift in my body. Was there a tingling in my fingers? A heaviness in my legs? My breath quickened as I searched for signs, terrified of what I might find.

I grew skilled at rationalizing everything away. A random bout of fatigue? I must not have gotten enough sleep. The occasional clumsiness? I was distracted. Is my body failing me? No, I am imagining things.

Even as I rationalized everything away, I remained on high alert. I became hyper-aware of every little twitch, every moment of weakness or dizziness. I wasn't living my life; I was monitoring it, waiting for something to go wrong. It was exhausting. I didn't realize how much energy I was pouring into trying to convince myself I was fine—or how little I was trusting my body.

One afternoon at the kitchen sink, a glass slipped from my hands. It shattered instantly, sending pieces skidding across the tile. My heart pounded. Had my fingers simply let go? Had I lost control of my grip? Todd came rushing in. "You okay?" I laughed, too quickly. "Yeah, I just got distracted." I bent down, scooping up the largest shards, careful to keep my face neutral. But I could still feel it—the dull slackness in my hand, the way it hadn't responded. My stomach churned. Some part of me knew. I rinsed my hands under cold water, pretending I was fine, willing the moment to pass.

Later, I replayed the moment in my head, analyzing it. Had I actually felt weak? Did my hand fail me, or was it merely a clumsy moment? And this was how it went. Every strange sensation, every misstep, every moment of forgetfulness became a test. Was this normal or was this MS?

As another month passed without incident, I convinced myself I was fine. I told myself I was in the clear, that whatever happened was behind me. Maybe it was nothing and the doctor was wrong. I held onto that one like a lifeline. The truth was, more than hoping, I was actively scanning for proof I was okay. Beneath the surface, the questions kept tugging. I wasn't ready to let go of the hope that I didn't have MS, so I continued to search for another story to believe in.

I scoured the internet for possible explanations that didn't involve MS, grasping onto anything that might prove my fears unfounded. One night, I stumbled across an article linking the flu shot to optic neuritis. And there it was again, the plausible explanation I had originally dredged up. A wave of relief washed over me. This must be the explanation. It made perfect sense, or at least it gave me something to hold onto—something that made the fear feel a little more manageable. And I clung to it, not because I was certain it was true, but because I needed it to be.

The longer I went without symptoms, the more I trusted the story I wanted to believe: that I had escaped. The doctor was wrong. For a time, it seemed like I was right. My MRIs stayed stable. No new symptoms, no warning signs. With each passing month, my confidence grew. Maybe it had been a fluke—an isolated incident never to be repeated. Maybe I was one of the lucky ones. Until I wasn't.

Strange how quickly the feeling of safety can crack open before your mind has time to catch up. The moment was so small, so ordinary, I almost ignored it. It was a typical Sunday morning, and Todd and I had decided to try a different church that day. The space was unfamiliar, but as we settled into the pews, something about it felt peaceful, even comforting.

The morning light streamed through the stained-glass windows, casting soft colors across the polished wood and illuminating the rich orange details near the altar. The pew beneath me was firm and grounding, solid in a way I hadn't realized I needed. The organ played, the choir's collective voice rose and swelled. In that moment, I felt steady—not because things were certain, but because something in me had let go.

I felt light. No worries pressing in, no fears gnawing at the edges of my mind. Just this quiet, ordinary moment. I let my shoulders relax into the pew, breathed in deeply, and allowed the music and sunlight to wash over me. I listened to the familiar cadence of the minister's voice, its gentle call to faith.

And as I shifted slightly in my seat, I noticed it. The tip of my right thumb felt strange—slightly dulled, not quite right. Small and dismissible, a flicker of oddness that should have meant nothing. I rubbed it absently, waiting for the sensation to return, expecting it to pass. But it didn't.

A slow, creeping awareness spread through me. *Oh, no.* I pressed my fingers together harder, willing the sensation back. *Oh my God, is this really happening?* I flexed my fingers, clenched my fist, testing, hoping. The numbness only deepened. It was real.

A familiar grip tightened around my chest, heavy and unrelenting. My breath hitched as I fidgeted in my seat. I forced my face into a mask of neutrality, but inside, panic clenched my ribs in a vice. After three years of convincing myself the specialist was wrong, of believing I was one of the lucky ones, I knew this feeling. I knew what it meant. This was the second episode. Ironically, what I prayed would never come happened while I was in church. In that moment, I didn't think about God. I didn't feel anger or comfort. It was more of an emotional bracing, like a shield snapping into place. I wasn't ready to fall apart. Not here. Not yet. So, I tucked the fear away and held myself still, pretending I was fine.

I swallowed hard, my throat tight and pulse quickening. Todd sat beside me, unaware, his head slightly bowed, his hands resting in his lap. Around us, the congregation murmured along with the minister's words. The world around me hadn't changed. But mine had.

What hit me first, even before the fear, was a strange sense of failure. For three years, I told myself if I did everything right, if I stayed positive enough, believed enough, willed it into existence, I could outrun this. As if I could bargain my way out of it through sheer determination. But what did that matter now? All that time convincing myself I was fine, and in the span of a single moment, I knew I wasn't.

I forced myself to sit still, to breathe, to pretend I was listening to the sermon. The minister's words faded into background noise, drowned out by the rush of thoughts colliding in my mind. *Is this just the beginning? How far will it spread? What if it never stops?* I willed myself to be wrong about what I was experiencing. Maybe I had just pinched a nerve.

Maybe...

I curled my fingers into a fist, holding them there, waiting, hoping. Nothing. I stared down at my hands in my lap, my vision tunneling. This was it, the moment I had feared. There was no denying it. And now I wasn't sure I could keep pretending I was fine.

By the next morning, the numbness had spread from my thumb into my entire right arm. I flexed my fingers and shook my wrist as I stood at the bathroom sink, watching my anxious reflection in the mirror. *Wake up. Please, wake up.* Nothing.

My stomach twisted as I pressed my palm flat against the cool granite countertop, testing my grip. It was still there, weak but functional. I could move my fingers, but the sensation was muted and dull, as if someone had wrapped my arm in layers of gauze. A lump rose in my throat. I tried rotating my shoulder and stretching my arm overhead, willing circulation back into it, but the heaviness remained, dense and unshakable.

I walked downstairs, forcing a smile as I kissed Carly and Lindsey good morning, moving through the routine as if nothing had changed. Todd was making coffee, the scent warm and familiar, grounding. Normal. Everything was normal. But it wasn't.

I carried plates to the table, my right hand unsteady, the fork slipping slightly from my grasp before I corrected it. Todd didn't notice. Was I imagining it? *Don't spiral. Just move on.*

The girls chatted brightly over their breakfast; oblivious their mother was quietly unraveling. I poured myself hot tea, cupping the mug in both hands, testing again. *Can I still hold it?* I could. That was good. That meant... what? That it wasn't as bad as I thought?

I took a sip, nodding along as Lindsey shared a story about school, my brain only half processing her words. Instead, I was hyperfocused on the sensations—or lack of them—in my right hand. Could I feel the heat of the mug as vividly as I should? Or was it fainter, distant, like a memory of warmth? I pressed my fingertips against the ceramic mug. I could feel its warmth. Good.

A low-level panic began to rise, clawing at the edges of my composure. I pushed the thought away. I wasn't ready to admit what this might mean. Instead, I needed to come up with new explanations like the pinched nerve. Or stress. Or the ever-hopeful *maybe it will be gone by tomorrow.*

The girls finished breakfast, and I moved through the rest of the morning on autopilot. Packing lunches, tying sneakers, brushing hair—every movement controlled, rehearsed, deliberate. The moment they were off to school, I exhaled, leaning against the counter, alone at last. Just me and the numbness.

As much as I did not want to admit it, that dull, heavy feeling was spreading. My ear and the right side of my face felt strange — thicker somehow. Doubt gnawed at me. *Should I call my neurologist? Admit what this might mean?* No. Not yet. I still needed a version of the story I could live with—one I could manage without breaking. So, I went with the safer orthopedic option: pinched nerve.

I made the appointment that afternoon, clinging to a fine thread of hope. But the moment I stepped into the waiting room, a brittle unease took hold. The air was sterile and cold, the kind of chill that settled into your skin. The stillness was broken by the tapping of computer keys and low voices drifting from behind the reception desk. Amid these ordinary sounds, my own tension felt oddly out of place. I rubbed my right arm absently, pressing my fingertips into my palm, testing. Still numb. Still wrong. And beneath the surface, my body mirrored my mind—tense, guarded, and bracing for news I didn't want to hear.

My mom was there with me, even though I hadn't told her everything I was afraid of. She didn't need the words. She could feel it. She sat beside me now, flipping through a magazine. Her movements were stiff, her fingers gripping the edges of the page. She didn't look at me—not directly, but I could feel the tension in her body, her energy anxiously buzzing. She didn't ask if I was okay, and somehow, that felt right.

I could feel her silent worry reaching toward me, and without thinking, I met it with steadiness—the way I always did when we were afraid together. I was the one who reassured her. I was the one who steadied the worry, made things feel manageable. Even now, with numbness creeping through my arm and fear tugging at the edges of my mind, my instinct was to protect her. So, I sat there, spine straight, voice even, and made sure I looked calm enough for both of us. On the outside, I appeared composed. Inside, I was pulled taut like a rubber band ready to snap.

There was also an unacknowledged ache rising from the space between us—years of worry and love, carried quietly, compressed into looks and careful words. I stood, rolled my shoulders, and shook out my hands as if I could release the restlessness. I kept telling myself: *It's just a pinched nerve. That's all it is.*

The orthopedic doctor was kind. With clinical efficiency, he asked questions as he worked, running me through a battery of tests. "Push against my hand," he instructed. I did. My muscles engaged, weak but functioning. "Good. Now, resist here." I pressed, feeling the pressure of his palm, the slight tremor in my own strength. "Close your eyes and touch your nose." I followed his command, but my movements felt clumsy, like my body and brain were out of sync. More tests. More instructions. I followed each one carefully, as if the right performance might lead to a gentler conclusion—anything but MS.

The doctor straightened up, gave a small nod. "Nothing concerning here. Probably just a pinched nerve. We'll run some more tests, but I don't think this is MS." Immediate relief bloomed, and I felt victorious. The orthopedic's words were my salvation: a confirmation of what I had been telling myself all along. I was fine. I was one of the lucky ones. The doctors had been wrong. I had been right, I told myself. All that worry in the church, all those nights lying in bed scanning my body for symptoms—it was all for nothing. I had almost let fear convince me of something terrible, but now, I could leave this whole MS scare in the past.

I smiled and thanked him, but as the relief settled over me, something small and sharp jabbed at me, creating a troubling feeling I couldn't shake. We weren't through yet; more tests were needed. The more tests he performed, and the more the results kept coming back normal, the less confident he grew. Finally, he stepped back, jotting a note down in my chart.

Something in his demeanor changed. It was barely perceptible, just a flicker across his face and the slightest hesitation in his voice. A small pause before he continued. "Let's get an MRI of the brain just to rule things out." And suddenly, the security I had wrapped myself in was slipping through my fingers. I couldn't quite process the words. They seemed to be floating out of reach. The room felt like it was closing in. A strange sense of injustice surged through me. How could he give me relief only to take it back? How could I be going from certainty to doubt again within a matter of minutes? I felt something inside me loosen, as if the floor quietly dropped out from under me.

The relief I had been holding onto until then evaporated. My stomach tightened. I wanted to believe he was being overly cautious, covering all bases, but deep down, I recognized it for what it was. This wasn't nothing. This wasn't going away, no matter how much I wanted to believe otherwise. A sense of certainty settled in, alerting me to what was coming.

I nodded, forcing myself to breathe, to stay composed. "Okay." But inside, I split into two versions of myself. One held on desperately to the denial I had built over the past three years. The other part of me, the one I had been trying to silence, was already sinking under the hidden truth.

I stood, nodded, and thanked the doctor, going through the motions. Inside, my mind was frantically trying to push away the truth as it edged closer. Walking back to the car, my mother's distress was a second presence beside me. We didn't speak. Her fear was palpable, and I felt the familiar pull to steady us both.

I started talking—fast, upbeat, too light. *"Well, it's just to be safe, right? I mean, doctors always do these tests to be thorough. It's probably nothing. I'll do the MRI, and then we'll never have to think about this again."*

It wasn't only her I was trying to convince. I was trying to convince myself. I could hear the forced brightness in my voice, but I didn't stop. Her worry was easier to manage, but the fear building inside me? That was another story. I kept talking, kept smiling, kept steadying her because the one thing I could not do was acknowledge the unfolding, undeniable truth: this ordeal was not over. Not even close.

A few days after the MRI, I was back in the orthopedist's office, sitting in the same chair, my hands pressed into the armrests a little tighter this time. The numbness had continued to spread, and I could no longer pretend it was nothing. Everything felt different now. The tentative relief I had carried out of our last appointment was nowhere to be found. Instead, a silent tension hung in the air between my mother and me. She may not have known how to talk about what was happening, but she was here—and that mattered.

I scanned the doctor's face as he flipped through the MRI results, searching for a sign of reassurance or an indication that this was all a formality. The look of apprehension in his eyes surfaced before he even spoke. I noticed the slight tightening of his jaw and the measured way he inhaled before choosing his next words. I braced myself.

"There are some areas of concern," he said, his voice carefully neutral. "It's best if you follow up with your neurologist."

The words landed, sharp and heavy. *Follow up with your neurologist.* The phrase hit with finality, leaving no room for denial.

I swallowed hard, trying to keep my voice even, "Concern about what?"

Another pause. "There are new lesions on your brain."

And there it was. I barely heard the rest. He was still talking, but I was drifting, untethered, like I had stepped outside my body and was watching the moment unfold from a distance. I nodded, not because I understood, but because nodding was the only thing keeping me grounded in that chair.

Lesions. New ones.

I had spent three years telling myself I was fine, that optic neuritis was an isolated glitch, not a warning sign. I clung to that version of the story like a life raft, rewriting the narrative again and again to keep fear at bay. But now, there was tangible, unavoidable proof. The hard truth lit up on an MRI screen, rendered in shades of gray and white.

My mind scrambled for other explanations, but none came. No more ifs or maybes. No more waiting. I was standing in the reality I had tried to outrun. And in that instant, something inside me buckled—a quiet breaking I couldn't hold off any longer. This was that second episode separated by space and time—the threshold I never wanted to cross.

My mother stiffened beside me as if reading my thoughts, her silence deafening. The orthopedic doctor leaned forward, his voice softer now. "I really think you need to make that appointment soon." I wanted to ask if soon meant urgent. If soon meant now. If soon meant my life was about to change. But I didn't. I just got up, nodded again, and willed myself to stay composed as I turned to leave.

In the car, the air was swarming with unspoken thoughts and feelings. I felt Mom watching me and waiting for some kind of reaction. Instead, I stared out the window as a hazy world passed by feeling the magnitude of what was to come. *I should call the neurologist. I should be scared.* Mostly, I felt numb.

My neurologist was in New York, so Todd and I took the Metro North into the city, the steady rhythm of the train a poor match for the chaos inside my head. Neither of us spoke much. What was there to say? We were heading toward an answer I dreaded but could no longer avoid.

Outside the window, buildings rose and fell in a dizzying pattern. I wasn't really seeing them. I was trapped between knowing and not knowing, between fear and hope, between the person I had been and the one I was about to become. I was busy replaying the past three years, still trying to convince myself this was a routine precaution and that maybe, somehow, there was yet another explanation. Such was the depth of my delusion.

The neurologist didn't waste time, and he did not sugarcoat his words. He had no bedside manner to speak of, but I excused this, telling myself I was seeing him for his expertise, not his demeanor.

"We need to do a spinal tap," he said, his voice steady and certain,. "That will give us the confirmation we need."

I heard the word *confirmation* louder than anything else. A gut punch. Then, *spinal tap*, the test I resisted and avoided for years, having convinced myself I didn't need it. Now, sitting across from the neurologist, I knew it was a step I could no longer avoid.

Hours later, I was curled on my side in a sterile exam room, knees drawn to my chest, trying to steady my breath as the doctor prepared for the procedure. The room was cold, the paper gown stiff against my skin. "This will feel like a pinch," he said.

A sharp, unnatural pressure shot through my lower back, a deep ache spreading outward like I was being hollowed out from the inside. I clenched my jaw, forcing myself to stay still. I focused on the rhythmic sound of my breath, the rise and fall of my own chest—returning to it again and again—anything to keep my mind from fixating on the slow pull of fluid being drained from my spine.

After the spinal tap, there would be no more guessing. I didn't yet know the results, but it felt as though my life was already beginning to split into before and after.

When it was over, I was instructed to lie flat to avoid a spinal headache. It came anyway, with a vengeance; a crushing, relentless pressure that made even the smallest movement unbearable. Todd and I checked into a nearby hotel since traveling home right away wasn't recommended. I was exhausted, drained in every possible way, but sleep eluded me. In the dim glow of the bedside lamp, my body felt heavy, my mind restless. *What if I had sealed my worst possible fate? Signed up for the confirmation of my deepest fear? What if wake up tomorrow and hear words that will change my life forever?* I turned onto my side, staring at the digital clock on the nightstand. The minutes trickled by, slow and relentless. There was nothing left to do now but surrender to it.

The days that followed were harder than the spinal tap itself. I had finally reached a point where I needed to know, one way or the other. I was ready for the truth. The waiting stretched on, day after day. It's strange how time crawls when you're waiting to hear what, deep down, you already know.

Days later, the phone rang. I almost didn't pick up. But I did. The words that had loomed over me for three years came through the line: *You have MS.* The words penetrated. I waited for the fear ever lurking in the back of my mind to surface, but it didn't come. Instead, a different emotion settled in its place: relief. Not because I wanted this diagnosis, but because the waiting was over. The not knowing, the uncertainty, the endless cycle of fear and denial all stopped in that instant. I could stop wondering now. I could stop questioning every little symptom and searching for answers just out of reach. Now I knew.

For three years, I lived with this possibility, braced for this moment. And now that it was here, I felt a strange, quiet certainty. This was what I had been preparing for, and I could handle it. I had to. And maybe I didn't have to do it all alone. Maybe the hardest truths are not meant to be carried in isolation, and healing begins the moment we stop trying to hold it all ourselves. The peace I felt in that moment was real—but it didn't last.

Later, Todd asked if I wanted to talk, but I didn't have the words yet. I wasn't ready to say it out loud, to give it form, because once I did, there was no taking it back. Instead, I sat in the quiet, breathing through the tightness in my chest, trying to find my footing in a world that had suddenly shifted beneath me.

After the girls were in bed that night, I sat alone in the dim light of the kitchen, staring at my untouched cup of tea. As I settled and processed the news, the enormity of the day pressed down on me. I now had clarity, a definitive answer, but as the silence settled around me, another truth emerged: This wasn't going away. That reality hit me in unrelenting waves. Now that I had a definitive diagnosis, what was I supposed to do with it? The question loomed, troublesome and unanswerable.

I spent years bargaining with God to let me be okay until the girls were older. Let me raise them. Let me see them off to college. And then, possibly, I could accept whatever was meant to come next. But now, there was no more bargaining. No more pretending this wasn't happening. It had already happened. I stood up, walked to the bathroom, and turned on the faucet. Cool water ran over my hands as I stared at myself in the mirror. My reflection stared back, unchanged, and yet, everything had changed.

What did all of this mean for me? For my family? For my future? I searched my eyes for an answer, perhaps some reassurance. Nothing. Just the apprehension of not knowing. I wasn't sure if I could do this, but at least I knew what I was dealing with. And for now, that was enough.

MS was here. No more what ifs, no more hoping I had outrun it. And now I had a choice: I could let the fear swallow me whole, or I could take the next step. I didn't know how to live with this yet, but I knew I had to start. The first step was to calm the widespread inflammation causing the numbness using high dose IV steroids. I was relieved to learn I would be receiving the infusions at the hospital rather than administering them myself at home. The last time—during the episode that took my vision—I had done the infusions alone, and managing the IV needle had been a constant source of anxiety. This time, at least I wouldn't have to go through that part alone.

Each morning after dropping the girls off at school, I drove myself to the hospital for treatment. The steroids left me anxious and sleep-deprived, my mind racing, and my body running on fumes. By the third morning, I was stuck between exhaustion and hyper-awareness, jittery from the medication yet trampled by a deep, cellular fatigue.

I moved through the morning routine on autopilot, making mini waffles with peanut butter for the girls, feeding the dogs, packing lunches. I was physically present but a million miles away. I wondered if the girls could sense me slipping further and further from myself. The normalcy of our routine was a thin, fragile veil that barely concealed my unraveling.

I hurried them into their car seats, my hands moving through familiar actions—buckling straps, tucking stray locks of hair behind their ears while my mind raced ahead to the day's treatment. I needed to get them to school, then get to the hospital, then....

CRASH.

I slammed on the brakes, my entire body lurching forward, but the impact was instantaneous, a sickening crunch that shattered through my brain fog. The sound hit first, violent and inescapable, and a half second later came the realization of what had transpired. My pulse spiked, breath catching in my throat. My hands gripped the steering wheel revealing white knuckles. I didn't want to turn around. I didn't want to see.

But I did.

In the rearview mirror, the gutters of our house dangled at an awkward angle, the siding torn, debris scattered across the driveway. My stomach dropped. My car. The house. The damage.

What did I just do?

For a moment, I sat frozen. The outside world continued as if nothing had happened. I glimpsed the neighbors pulling out of their driveway and birds chirping in the early morning light. But inside the car, inside my body, everything had stopped.

The girls!

I turned sharply; my breath trapped somewhere in my chest. "Are you okay?" My voice was high and bright, the forced calm of a mother trying to keep her anxiety from spilling over. Carly and Lindsey's wide eyes blinked back at me. "Mommy, what happened?" Carly asked, her voice small. I swallowed hard, forcing a wobbly smile. "It's okay, sweetheart." But my words felt thin, stretched over a moment too big to contain.

I climbed out of the car on shaking legs. The damage was worse up close. The impact had left a deep dent in the car, and the back bumper was pushed awkwardly inward. Pieces of the house lay scattered across the driveway; shattered bits of wood and plastic, remnants of what, only moments ago, were solid and whole.

My stomach twisted. How was I going to tell Todd I drove our new car into our newly re-sided home? *How did I do this?* To this day, we still can't quite figure it out.

I knelt down, pressing my hands to my knees, trying to steady my rapid, shallow breaths. A wave of nausea rolled through me. The steroids already had me on edge, and now the adrenaline was flooding my system, leaving my body jittery and unsteady. I felt like I was vibrating from the inside out. *Pull yourself together. The girls still need to get to school.*

I forced myself to get back in the car. My hands trembled on the steering wheel as I backed out— carefully, hyperaware of every movement. I opted for the stop-kiss-and-drop line instead of parking and walking them in, knowing I didn't have it in me to answer casual questions or pretend nothing was wrong. I kissed them both and told them to have a good day. They nodded, but their eyes lingered on me, uncertain. I could feel the worry they didn't yet have words for.

As I drove toward the hospital for my infusion, the reality of what happened pressed in. I had crashed my car. Into our house. Not because I was distracted. Not because I was careless. But because I wasn't fully *here*. My body was operating in one reality while my mind was trapped in another. Everything I had been carrying—the diagnosis, the steroids, the fear I was trying so hard to suppress— finally caught up with me.

By the time I pulled into the hospital parking lot, it all collapsed in on me. I turned off the car and sat there, staring blankly at the dashboard. My hands, still gripping the wheel, felt like they didn't belong to me. Finally, the floodgates opened. Sobs tore through me, raw and uncontrollable. The kind of crying that comes from somewhere deeper than sadness. The kind that rises up from exhaustion, fear, and the intolerable strain of pretending to be okay for far too long.

I wasn't okay. I was afraid. And even though I wasn't truly alone, I had been carrying it all inside—trying to stay strong, to keep moving, to manage it all on my own. I had told myself that if I just kept it together, maybe it wouldn't all catch up to me. But it had, and I couldn't hold it all anymore.

I wasn't alone—support was there—but I hadn't yet learned how to feel safe asking for help. I was still trying to protect the people I loved from my pain, still clinging to the belief that needing support made me a burden. Deep down, I feared that if I truly let someone see the depth of my fear and exhaustion, it would be too much on them.

That day, after telling Todd the news that I had accidentally backed the car into the house, the thought of asking for more felt impossible. Not because he wouldn't have been there—but because I didn't yet know how to let him. Our marriage was still young. We hadn't yet done the work we've done since to hold space for the hard things. In that moment, calling a friend felt like a gentler place to begin—a small, safer step toward daring to believe I didn't have to carry this alone.

With shaky fingers, I reached for my phone and dialed her number. "Can you come?" I whispered. And when she came and sat beside me in stillness without needing to fix or minimize anything—a part of me softened. The weight I had carried for years lifted. I let myself be seen, and nothing shattered, the world didn't collapse. Instead, I felt held. It was the beginning of something new—a fragile kind of trust that I could ask for help and still be loved. I no longer had to be invincible to be worthy.

That moment became a turning point, not only in how I related to others, but how I related to myself. Since then, I've continued to learn that letting people in doesn't make me weak—it allows me to be more fully human. It deepens connection, creates space for honesty, and reminds me I don't have to do any of this alone. I'm still learning to trust—to ask, to receive, to believe I'm not too much. And each time I do, life grows more spacious, more tender, more real. I'm reminded, again and again, that allowing myself to be truly supported is in itself healing.

I still don't know what the future holds, but I'm not resisting it anymore. I'm meeting it with less armor and a little more grace.

Pause and Reflect

- Have you ever experienced a moment where waiting for the unknown felt harder than the truth itself? What was that experience like for you? If you knew what was coming, how did knowing, whether good news or bad, change your perspective?

- When faced with uncertainty, do you tend to hold everything in, or do you reach out for support? What has been your instinct in challenging times, and how has it served you? If asking for help is difficult, what might it feel like to take a small step toward allowing support?

- Is there a moment in your life where you felt like the weight of everything crashed down on you? How did you respond in that moment? Looking back, is there anything you wish you had done differently to care for yourself?

- Who are the people in your life you feel safe leaning on? If no one comes to mind, what kind of support would feel most meaningful to you? How can you take a step toward finding that support?

- What does 'stepping into the future' mean to you right now? Whether facing a diagnosis, a major life transition, or an unknown ahead, how might you move forward with more presence and self—compassion?

Part Two:
Lessons from a Teacher in Disguise

5

THE POWER OF LETTING GO

"You don't think your way into a new kind of living. You live your way into a new kind of thinking." — Henri Nouwen

There is a moment in every journey when the real work begins — not the work of fighting or fixing, but the sacred work of letting go. It's the kind that lives in the uncomfortable spaces between fear and surrender. For me, that moment didn't arrive all at once. It came slowly, in layers. In the choices I made—not to push harder, but to soften. Not to grip, but to release.

I used to think letting go meant losing control. That if I stopped managing, explaining, proving—everything I feared would catch up with me. The uncertainty. The illness. The feeling that if I didn't hold it all together, everything might fall apart. And underneath it all, I was afraid that if I let go—if people saw the messy, vulnerable parts of me—I'd be judged or rejected.

At first, letting go didn't feel like relief, it stirred up fear. But what I have learned is that letting go requires a kind of courage. It is choosing trust over control. It is whispering to yourself, *I don't have to hold all of this alone anymore.*

I began to release the version of myself as the person who could do it all—the woman who never asked for help and believed her worth came from being everything to everyone. The perfect wife, mother, daughter, friend. The one who hosted the holidays, planned the birthdays, ran the playdates, and made it all look effortless. And when I couldn't keep up that pace—when my body started saying no—I felt lost. Who was I if I wasn't that person anymore? Yet, in letting her go, I began to uncover someone softer, someone more authentic.

In the early years of living with MS, I spent a lot of time trying to control it. I told myself that if I did everything "right," I could keep it at bay. I dove into research, especially around diet and self-care, and structured my days around things that felt proactive—exercise, massage, meditation, supplements, and journaling. I started therapy to help with the deeper work of learning to say no, and understanding why disappointing others felt almost unbearable.

At the time, dietary protocols for MS were widely discussed, many of them emphasizing strict rules around food and the avoidance of certain ingredients. On the surface, this didn't feel too difficult for me—I was already a "healthy eater." Or so it appeared.

Those rigid approaches bypassed my desire for wellness and tapped into something deeper. They gave me permission to restrict, to control, to do something that looked disciplined on the outside, even as it drained me on the inside.

Later, I encountered another highly structured approach, promoted through a compelling personal recovery story and framed as a path back to health through disciplined eating. It was tempting—proof, perhaps, that if I followed the rules closely enough, I could fix this.

But the rigidity was intense. For someone already carrying a complicated relationship with food, it quickly became more harmful than helpful. Looking back, I can see how my desire to manage MS quietly reawakened old beliefs and behaviors. The restrictions weren't just about food—they became a way to feel in control. A way to do something right.

And people praised me for it—praised me for being thin, for having "so much willpower." They always had.

But beneath the surface, something else was happening. I was following the rules about what to cut out, but I wasn't nourishing myself with what I actually needed. Not just physically, but emotionally—I wasn't letting myself be held, supported, or truly seen. Deep down, I think a part of me knew this wasn't just about being healthy. But admitting that would have meant facing how easily the old patterns had crept back in. How familiar—and falsely comforting—control still felt. At that point in my life, I wasn't ready to hold that truth. Not yet.

What was meant to be healing soon became a source of stress, shame, and physical decline. I felt confused and defeated. I had tried so hard to do everything right—to control my MS, to control my body. But the more I tried to control, the more I suffered. I learned the hard way that what heals one person might harm another, and following someone else's path does not guarantee the same outcome. Chasing perfection, especially when disguised as healing, can become its own form of suffering.

Over the years, therapy has helped me dismantle the beliefs that kept me stuck, like having to be everything for everyone, or thinking that resting is a sign of weakness, and that saying "no" made me a selfish person. Therapy is where I learned to set boundaries without guilt, to feel my feelings without shame, and to grieve the life I thought I was supposed to live. More than anything, it helped me relate to myself with greater compassion and forgiveness. I had spent so long trying to be kind to everyone else, and therapy helped me realize I too deserved that same kindness.

As I learned to care for myself differently, I began to care a little less about what others thought of me. I found I needed less external validation. I was slowly learning how to offer myself the grace I had been waiting to receive from others.

Over time, therapy became more than emotional support, it became a vital part of my healing. Having a safe place to process my experiences, explore my fears, and be fully seen has supported not only my emotional well-being, but also my physical health. My neurologist and neuropsychiatrist both concur that my commitment to therapy has likely played an important role in helping me stay steady—physically and emotionally—as I navigate life with chronic illness.

Caring for myself means more than tending to emotions, it also means making decisions about my physical health. When I was first diagnosed, going on a disease-modifying medication seemed like the obvious choice. I was scared and overwhelmed, and in a world where so little felt within my control, it gave me a sense of taking action. It felt like my insurance policy— a personal attempt to protect myself from the fear that MS might one day ask more of me than I was ready to give.

Over time, the decision to take medication became harder to embrace. There were side effects to consider, and risks to weigh, alongside stories of people managing their MS without medication. I started to question everything. I went back and forth—afraid to stay on, afraid to go off. Beneath it all was a sense of shame that I might be doing something wrong by relying on medicine instead of trusting my body or choosing a more natural path. Everyone had an opinion, and depending on who I spoke to, the "right" choice seemed to shift.

For a long time, I didn't fully trust my own voice. I was often a product of the last conversation I'd had—desperately trying to do what I thought was best, even when it pulled me away from what I truly needed. Over time, I began to relate to medication differently—not as a failure or a solution, but as one possible form of care. Sometimes it felt steadying, sometimes it felt fraught, but each choice came from the same place: *I'm scared, and I'm doing the best I can with what I know right now.*

What helped me find steadiness wasn't only medication; it was also the way I was learning to relate to myself. That's where I began learning how to stay with myself.

The practice of being mindful helped me decipher those voices—both around me and inside me. It taught me how to meet myself where I was, with compassion instead of judgment. It showed me that I could change my mind. I didn't have to get it perfectly right; I could make the choice that felt right in that moment. And if things changed, I could choose again. Learning to trust myself in this way brought a deep sense of relief.

That growing self-trust also required honesty about how I was really doing. That didn't come naturally to me. I had spent most of my life trying to appear fine, even when I wasn't—partly to protect the people I loved, and partly because I learned that being strong, cheerful, and composed made me easier to love. I also learned early on that anything messy or uncertain—especially illness—was something to hide. Over time, I came to believe that showing pain made others uneasy, and that it was better to pretend I was okay.

That belief ran deep. Vulnerability felt like a risk I couldn't afford. So, when MS entered my life, it collided with everything I thought made me acceptable. Being visibly unwell didn't just feel like weakness, it felt like something that might change how others saw me—not as strong or capable, but as fragile, or worse, a burden. I feared I would be seen as too much, as less than, and not enough all at the same time.

My father taught me the power of positive thinking, and for that, I'll always be grateful. But I also learned to use positivity as a shield. I used it to keep others comfortable and to avoid sitting with my feelings of fear, anger, grief, or sadness.

At times, I smiled when I didn't feel like smiling. I brushed off pain with phrases like, "It'll be fine," or "At least it's not worse." I used my upbeat attitude as armor, not realizing I was bypassing the feelings that needed my attention.

What I have come to know is this: the feelings we avoid don't disappear. They wait. And they often return as physical symptoms, anxiety, or the exhaustion we try to ignore. It took time to recognize the signs my body was trying to send me. For years, and even now when I become overwhelmed or overstimulated, old symptoms can temporarily return. My vision might blur, numbness may creep in, and fatigue can tighten its grip. I used to see these symptoms as signs of something wrong—as threats that my body was failing me. Mindfulness gave me a new lens. As I slowed down and paid closer attention, I noticed something remarkable: those symptoms became signals. Invitations to pause. To listen. To care for myself before things escalated. And when I did? The symptoms often receded.

Even now, all these years later, I still struggle with rigid, tight muscles—my body's way of gripping in the face of stress and tension. Of holding on. But I continue to meet it with curiosity and kindness. I continue to try, through breath and stillness, to teach my body what my heart is slowly learning: it is safe to let go.

Letting go also meant learning to disappoint others—without abandoning myself. There was a moment I'll never forget. It wasn't dramatic or life-altering on the surface, but at the time, something inside me shifted and I've carried it with me ever since. We had plans to go to dinner at a friend's house, but that day, the MS fatigue hit with a vengeance. Not regular tiredness but a deep, cellular exhaustion that swallows you whole. I knew with every fiber of my being that I couldn't go. I called to let my friend know. I tried to be honest, and I thought she'd understand, but my words were met with confusion and subtle disbelief. I could feel her disappointment, maybe even frustration. Her reaction wasn't cruel, it was human, but it broke something open in me.

I spent years trying to explain, to justify, to be understood. That night, I saw the cost—not only of missing dinner, but of all the times I silenced my needs to preserve someone else's comfort. All the time I had pushed through when I needed rest or said *yes* while my body screamed *no*. And I felt sad. Sad that I couldn't go. Sad that she didn't understand. Sad that something as ordinary as making it to dinner with friends was so out of reach.

That night, I realized that not everyone would come with me on this journey. Some friendships would change, and some might fall away. But I also grasped something else: if I was going to live well with MS, I had to stop forsaking myself to make others comfortable. I had to stop putting their feelings above my needs.

That night, I began to let go. Not just of that one dinner, but also of the belief that I had to be everything for everyone in order to be loved. It didn't happen all at once. Letting go, I've learned, is something you practice—again and again. Some days it comes easily. Other days, I still feel the tug to explain, to prove, to be heard. But now I try to meet that tug with tenderness. I remind myself that choosing me isn't selfish. It's how I stay well and whole.

It can still feel scary to use my voice—to speak up when I fear it might disappoint someone. My default is to hold things in, to try not to be a burden. Mindfulness and therapy have helped me see how much that costs me. It's only through practice—small moments of honesty, of naming what I need, of sharing what I'm feeling—that I've learned I don't have to go through hardship in a void. Each time I let someone in and was met with warmth instead of distance, I felt a bit safer, a little more seen. I learned that real connection is possible, but only when we allow ourselves to be truly known. And in those moments, I found strength, relief, ease, peace, and hope. I discovered I could do hard things, and I didn't have to do them alone.

While letting go was difficult, especially the ache of shedding old roles and relationships, it was also clarifying. It helped me see who could meet me where I really was. And it allowed me to show up—not just for the people who mattered, but for myself.

Letting go didn't only mean saying no to others, it meant saying yes to myself in ways that once felt loaded with shame. That included my relationship with anxiety medication. For years, I thought needing it meant I was somehow failing—that if I was strong enough, grounded enough, mindful enough, I wouldn't need help.

Over time, that belief began to soften.

I've come to see medication as one part of how I sometimes care for myself. For someone like me with a highly sensitive nervous system, it helps regulate what can otherwise feel overwhelming. Amid the noise and chaos of daily life, even the most ordinary moments can feel like too much: a simple conversation in a crowded room, a bright overhead light, too many tabs open in my mind. The medication doesn't take it all away, but it helps lessen the intensity so I can stay steady. It gave me just enough space to meet my experience, rather than be swept away by it. Even now, those same sensitivities remain. I just meet them with more awareness and a little more compassion.

During those early years of overwhelm, I deepened my mindfulness practice. I woke early each morning to meditate and I did a body scan at night. I tried, when I remembered, to stay present in between. These weren't just routines, they became lifelines.

Mindfulness helped me stay connected to myself when everything around me was spinning out of control. It helped me let go of what I couldn't fix, like others' reactions, the course of MS, and the unpredictability of life. It taught me I could choose how I responded, how I treated myself, and how I showed up. These shifts didn't only change my internal world; they also began to ripple outward into my relationships.

One evening, years ago, Todd returned home from a business trip and noticed I hadn't gone to the store to get his usual deli meat and cheese. He was disappointed and frustrated, and in the moment, his reaction overwhelmed me. Before, I might have collapsed inward, swallowed my feelings, or even snapped back. But that night, I sat with the discomfort. I meditated. I reminded myself I was safe. Instead of spiraling into fear or shame, I remained in the present. From that grounded place, I went to him—not in anger, but with vulnerability—and shared how his reaction affected me. What followed was an honest and healing conversation. It wasn't about the cheese at all—it was about his own need to feel considered and cared for. And because I stayed with myself, we could see each other more clearly.

Moments like that accumulated. My practice evolved. It became less about what happened on the cushion, and more about how I moved through the world. It emerged as less of a discipline and more of a lifestyle: a steady, quiet companion that helped me heal—not just within myself, but in my relationships too.

Most importantly, mindfulness anchored me in the present. It helped ease the fear by teaching me to relate to it differently—reminding me that in this moment, I was okay. Even when things were hard, I could say: *I can meet this. I am not alone. I will be okay.* That gave me something real and steady to hold on to.

I grew less reactive and more grounded. I savored small joys like curling up with my girls to read and breathing in the warmth of their freshly washed hair. I'd watch Carly twirl her fingers through her hair, thumb in mouth, while Lindsey looped the frayed ribbon of her beloved stuffed pig, Piggy, around her wrist like a bracelet. These ordinary moments became sacred. Not despite my limitations, but because of them. I wasn't living in fear of the next relapse I was learning to live more fully in the present moment.

Others noticed, too. Friends said I looked different, lighter somehow. People were drawn to something they couldn't quite name. On the days I felt off, overwhelmed, or impatient, my daughters, still so little, would gently say, "Mommy didn't meditate today." They could feel the difference. That subtle transformation was the start of something new. I didn't know it then, but I was beginning to reshape my life from the inside out. The practices that helped me feel more grounded and whole were laying the groundwork for something new—seeds of steadiness, presence, and ease that would continue to grow in ways I couldn't yet imagine.

Here is what I've come to know about mindfulness and letting go: *The practice is not about getting it right. It is a place to land. A way of meeting yourself exactly where you are.*

Letting go is not something you do once. It is something you choose over and over. It's not weakness. It's wisdom. It's not the end of strength—it is the beginning of grace. Most of all, it's how we find our way back to ourselves.

Letting go is often seen as an act of release, but it is just as much an act of return. A return to your truth. Your needs. Your breath. Your being.

I still fall off track. I still get caught in fear, in tension, and in the pressure to perform, but I return to myself again and again. That's the work. That's the path.

As you move through illness, uncertainty, or even everyday transitions, letting go may not always feel graceful. It might feel shaky, emotional, or even lonely, but letting go doesn't mean abandoning who you are. It means making room for who you're becoming.

Each time you lean into rest instead of pushing through... Each time you ask for support instead of holding it all in... Each time you choose truth over performance... You are not losing ground. You are reclaiming it. You are coming back to the place inside you that has always known you are worthy. You are enough. You matter.

This path, this practice isn't just about letting go. It's about learning to feel safe within yourself. To feel worthy without earning it. To stop performing for love and finally receive it simply by being who you *are*.

Pause and Reflect

- What does "letting go" mean to you right now? Is there something you're trying to control that may be asking to be released?

- Have you ever equated rest or asking for help with weakness? Where do you think that belief came from—and how is it serving (or hurting) you today?

- Can you recall a moment when your body gave you a signal you initially ignored? What did that moment teach you in hindsight?

- Are there roles or expectations you have outgrown but still cling to? What might it feel like to loosen your grip?

- How can you create a gentler, more supportive relationship with yourself? What does true self-care look like for you, not the Instagram version, but the soul-level kind?

- What relationships feel aligned with who you're becoming—and which ones may be asking for new boundaries or gentle release?

- What is one small way you can practice letting go today—without abandoning yourself?

6

Trusting My Inner Wisdom

"The soul often speaks through longing, and the wisdom of our desire is greater than we know." — Sue Monk Kidd

There was a time when I believed the answers I needed lived outside of me—in experts, books, research studies, and well-meaning advice. And for a while, that belief served me. It gave me something to hold onto in the uncertainty of life with MS. But over time, I began to hear something else—a quieter voice beneath the noise. My own.

Learning to trust that voice didn't happen overnight. It came slowly— through trial and error, with practice, and through the gentle unfolding of something I hadn't realized I'd been missing: self-trust. I never noticed how much I relied on others to tell me what was best for me—my insightful, observant husband saw it before I did.

Todd used to say, half-joking and half-concerned, that I was "the product of my last conversation." At first, I bristled. But when I stepped back and noticed my own patterns, I saw the truth of his words. If my neurologist recommended a specific medication, I leaned into it. If I later came across an article about a promising diet protocol, I'd go that route. I would go on medication, then off, then back on again. My decisions changed with the winds of outside influence. I kept placing trust in what others believed was best for me without realizing I was losing touch with what I believed.

Through mindfulness, I found my way back to myself. As I deepened my practice, I came to hear my own voice more clearly. I grew to rely on inner clarity rather than external approval. I stopped asking, "What is the right answer?" and learned to ask something far more compassionate: *What feels true for me right now?* That one perceptual shift transformed my thinking and behavior.

I started to relax around decisions. I no longer needed to find the perfect answer—I only needed to choose what I felt aligned with in the moment and trust I could change course if needed. That realization brought a deep, unexpected peace. I didn't have to force certainty. I only had to listen inward.

This shift also eased my lifelong need to please others. For years I was like a chameleon, readily adapting to the values of the people around me. When I was with those who believed in medication, I felt confident in my decision to take it. When I spent time with people who believed only in natural healing, I felt ashamed of that same choice. My sense of direction was constantly swaying, but over time, I rooted myself in my own truth.

The reality is, I had relapses both on and off medications. I had relapses both on and off MS diets. I don't know for sure whether the medications or diets helped or not. No one does. That's the thing about chronic illness: we crave definitive answers, but often, we're asked to live in the unknown.

Multiple sclerosis is often described as a chronic, autoimmune disease of the central nervous system—but those words have never fully captured what it means to live with it. For me, MS has been defined less by any single symptom and more by its unpredictability. It can be quiet for long stretches and then flare without warning. A body that feels steady one day can feel unfamiliar the next. There are no clear rules, no guarantees—only patterns noticed in hindsight and choices made without certainty. Living with MS has meant learning to coexist with not knowing, even as I longed for answers.

Living in the unknown was never comfortable for me. I longed for certainty, something solid to hold on to. That longing often pulled me toward strict protocols and promises of control, but instead of peace, it led to more suffering. What I do know is when I obsessed over finding the "perfect" solution—when I lived in fear, restriction, and control—I agonized more. Every major relapse came on the heels of a significant stressor. My body held it together during the crisis but collapsed in the aftermath. It wasn't about being perfect with a protocol. It was about how much stress I was carrying and how disconnected I was from myself.

The more I learned to quiet the noise, the more I found calm amid the uncertainty. I grew more confident in decisions that others questioned. Sometimes my neurologist disagreed. Sometimes I would not comply with what a naturopath asked of me. And still, I held my ground in spite of the emotional discomfort— not to be difficult, but because I was finally learning to trust myself.

Eventually, I stopped asking, *what is the right treatment?* and started asking, *what choice will bring me the most peace? What step will help me stay grounded and present in the life I want to live?*

Moments of self-trust did not just occur in doctor's offices or with big decisions, they happened in everyday life too. Like saying yes to a slice of ice cream cake at a birthday party. In earlier years, I might have declined, afraid it wasn't "on the plan." But over time, I noticed how much joy lived in those little moments. Skipping the cake made me feel deprived and disconnected. Saying yes brought delight, presence, and connection. It reminded me that joy and belonging were just as essential to my well-being as any protocol.

There were times when friends, practitioners, or family members offered advice that didn't feel right. In the past, I would have doubted myself, but mindfulness helped me pay attention to my body's responses. When a decision was aligned with my truth, I felt peaceful. When it wasn't, I felt uneasy. That secure feeling of peace became my compass. Trusting myself didn't mean I stopped seeking guidance, it just meant I knew the final say was mine.

Learning to follow that compass did not only guide my choices—it also changed the way I experienced the world around me. It made me more attuned to my own sensitivity, especially as MS heightened the impact of stress and emotion on my body. I have always been a sensitive person—easily moved, easily affected—but MS brought that sensitivity to the surface in new ways. Too much noise overwhelmed me. Lack of sleep or changes in temperature threw me off. But the kind of stress that unsettled me most wasn't physical, it was emotional.

Relational tension hit me the hardest. If someone close to me was upset, I not only felt sad, I felt unwell. My body reacted. Over time, I realized these symptoms were not random, they were signals. They were asking me to pause and care for myself, but instead I often pushed through. I had grown up thinking that strength meant setting my needs aside for the sake of others.

At first, I resisted the very idea of putting my needs first. I didn't want to disappoint anyone or appear selfish. I didn't want to need rest. I had internalized the belief that strength meant having it all together—that good mothers, good daughters, good women didn't need rest, didn't say no, and were always supposed to be calm and in control. I equated being strong with being selfless, tireless, and endlessly capable. Rest did not fit that image.

Eventually, the warnings from my body became signals I could no longer dismiss. When your vision blurs, half your body goes numb, or your nervous system feels like it is short-circuiting, you can't just push through. You have to stop. You have to listen. That's when I began to see MS as a teacher—one that sure got my attention.

Mindfulness helped me reframe the story I told myself about my body: it wasn't betraying me; it was guiding me. Each symptom was a message asking for care and compassion. As I began to listen, my body offered simple answers, truths I had ignored for far too long:

Rest

Let your voice be heard.

Set a boundary.

Let yourself be seen.

Remember that you matter.

And slowly, as I honored these messages, my voice—the one I silenced —started to come back.

This journey has been, in many ways, about reclaiming my voice. About taking up space. About believing that I matter, my needs matter, my voice matters. The more I abandoned myself to avoid conflict or gain approval, the louder MS shouted. When I honored my needs by speaking up, slowing down, or reaching out for support, my body responded in kind, and MS sometimes loosened its grip on me.

Now, when those familiar symptoms start to surface, I pause and ask *what am I not saying? What is it I need that I'm not giving myself?* Sometimes it's rest. Sometimes it's connection or courage or a hard "no." Every time I honor those needs, I return to myself a little more.

One of the greatest challenges of getting in touch with your truth, is learning to distinguish fear from intuition. Sometimes fear yells so loudly it sounds like truth. Sometimes intuition is only a whisper. I have come to learn that they register differently in my body. Fear is tight, anxious, reactive—it pushes. Intuition is quieter, steadier—it guides.

Mindfulness helped me begin to notice those differences, but sometimes the noise inside was still too loud to sort through on my own. That's where therapy became another anchor for me—a space to slow down, untangle my thoughts, and hear myself more clearly. Therapy gave me space to pause and listen for the differences between fear and intuition. Like meditation, it offered a place where I didn't have to be strong—a place to unravel, reflect, and reconnect with my own voice. When I felt unsure, I sat with each option and noticed how it landed in my body and heart. Over time, and with the compassionate presence of my therapist, that soft, sure voice became easier to hear and easier to trust.

A growing sense of inner safety didn't just help me navigate emotions—it influenced how I approached treatment options.

Mindfulness taught me to stop outsourcing and begin consulting myself. I still gathered information from others, but I learned to discern what was best for me. What helped most was knowing I didn't have to get it perfect. No decision was permanent. I could make the best choice for now—and if I needed to pivot, I could.

My body became my guide. When I sat with a decision, I paid attention to how I felt. Tightness or anxiety? That was fear. Spaciousness or ease? That was intuition. After deciding, I used my body as feedback. If I felt unsettled, I paused and revisited. If I felt peace, I trusted I had chosen well. Letting my body guide me kept me grounded in hard moments. That is the gift of inner wisdom— it is not always loud, but it is consistent. Despite this newfound clarity, there were times I overrode my own knowing—especially when I placed the needs of others above my own.

One of the most humbling moments occurred at a time when my client schedule was jam-packed. I was holding space for so many others, each with their own tender stories, when I felt my nervous system start to fray. Their pain touched places in me that were still healing. I left sessions feeling raw and depleted but told myself I should be able to manage. It was the first time I realized my own unhealed pain was affecting my ability to stay present for others—and how deeply I needed care, too.

Eventually, I reached a breaking point. My body and mind were waving every red flag they could, and I couldn't keep pretending I was fine. Stepping away from client work wasn't easy—it tore at me. I worried I was letting people down, leaving them without the support they deserved. But the truth was, I wasn't in a place to help clients. I was running on empty, struggling more than anyone knew, and needing the same care I urged others to give themselves.

Abiding by that realization was excruciating, but necessary. That experience taught me a hard lesson in self-trust: sometimes the truth you most need to honor is the one you most wish to avoid. And choosing yourself is the most responsible choice you can make, despite feeling like you are failing someone else.

Essentially, trusting yourself means honoring the quiet wisdom inside you—even when it asks you to stop, to let go, or to step back from something you so want to hold on to. I had to admit I wasn't living what I taught and that a depleted mindfulness coach isn't of service to anyone. As painful as it was, that moment was a turning point. It reminded me that self-trust takes courage—the kind that listens deeply and chooses what is needed, although it may be the hardest choice to make. Ultimately, trusting yourself is not about always getting it right. It's about being willing to listen. Willing to soften. Willing to begin again, as many times as you need to.

Pause and Reflect

- When have you sought answers outside of yourself instead of turning inward? What effect did that have on you?

- Can you recall a time when honoring your inner wisdom brought a sense of peace or clarity? Did it come naturally or did you have to work to build that inner trust in yourself?

- What does the voice of fear sound like in your body and how is it different from the voice of intuition?

- What is one small way you can begin to trust yourself more today? How might you remind yourself of this intention throughout the day?

7

STRESS, MINDFULNESS, AND HEALING

"Feelings come and go like clouds in a windy sky. Conscious breathing is my anchor." — Thich Nhat Hanh

Living with MS means living with a nervous system that sometimes misfires—without warning, without logic, without pause.

There were times when ordinary sounds startled me—my children's voices, the clatter of dishes, the buzz of daily life. Everything seemed to be turned up too loud. I couldn't focus. Sometimes it felt like my brain was short-circuiting— sparks flying and every connection misfiring. I was left incapable of catching a single thought. When someone spoke to me, their words seemed distant and jumbled. Like a message traveling through static, the meaning slipped away before I could grasp it.

That mental static was not only in my head; it also weighed on every part of me, putting my body on high alert. My muscles ached from constant tension, my stomach was often in knots, and sleep was elusive. But it was the sensory overwhelm—the inability to think clearly, to pause, to catch my breath—that left me feeling scattered and, at times, disconnected. In those moments, the simplest requests felt like too much. My nervous system was overloaded, and I didn't yet have the tools to unburden it.

Living in that state day after day wore me down, and overload turned into chronic stress. It didn't live in just one corner of my life— the stress settled into my body, my thoughts, my relationships. It created distance between me and the people I loved, making it harder to truly listen or show up the way I wanted to.

Before I began to relate to stress differently, I spent countless hours worrying about the future. *Would I become disabled? What would that look like for our family? Would I be able to care for our daughters, or would I become a burden?* When fear had me spinning in a loop of uncertainty, it pulled me further from the present moment. I might be sitting on the floor playing with the girls, but my mind was miles away, tangled in what-ifs.

Being in a constant state of fear and tension eventually showed up in my body as tight shoulders, clenched jaw, shallow breath. And the tension only grew and made my MS symptoms impossible to ignore. My vision blurred, numbness returned with a thick, weighted sensation, and dizziness struck if I moved my head too fast. The "short-circuited" feeling in my brain intensified. So did my anxiety—sometimes tipping me into panic.

When the overwhelm flared, I often withdrew into myself, stepping back from Todd, the girls, even friends who cared deeply—not because I wanted distance, but because I was scared to need too much from anyone. The thought of asking for help felt foreign, almost impossible. I couldn't have expressed what I needed; I only knew I didn't want to feel so alone. But that felt hard to say out loud. So, I withdrew. I didn't know how to show others the parts of me that felt so raw and unsteady. The parts that needed care. The parts I wasn't yet in touch with. Being vulnerable felt risky. What if it was too much? What if *I* was too much? It was easier to stay quiet. To hold it in. To carry on as if I was fine. But deep down, I wasn't fine. I just didn't know how to ask for what I needed.

Stress also fed my perfectionism and people-pleasing. I'd push myself past exhaustion trying to meet everyone's expectations or avoid disappointing them, even at the cost of my own well-being. Rather than rest, I'd kick into overdrive and reorganize the pantry, purge the closets, tackle every drawer in the house. One project bled into the next. Busyness became a coping strategy, a way to feel in control. There was something oddly soothing about staying busy—if I could just keep moving, I might stay ahead of the unraveling. But what I truly needed wasn't more doing—it was permission to pause, to rest, and to simply be. Underneath the productivity was a body screaming for relaxation, a mind desperate for peace, and a heart longing for care and compassion.

My body could only carry so much stress before it cried out for relief. And when it did cry out, the illusion of control slipped through my fingers, leaving me exposed to the fear I was trying hard to outrun. Like the time I was in New York, shopping with my mom, something we had often done together and always enjoyed. We were riding the escalator down to the main floor of Saks Fifth Avenue, where the air buzzed with noise and motion. As we descended, the scene below blurred. A familiar uneasiness crept in—tightness in my chest, a rush of lightheadedness, hands beginning to tremble. I feared my legs might give out beneath me. And then came the dread—the recognition that *this* was happening again. I was slipping into panic. Trapped in my own skin, I was desperate to escape, but unsure how or who to ask for help.

Panic took over. I found myself unable to tell my mom what was happening. Recognizing it as a panic attack, and not a medical emergency, did not make it any less frightening. The crush of the crowd intensified the anxiety. I needed something cold to drink. I needed air.

I made an excuse to step outside and found a street vendor on the corner. I bought a bottle of water and took a few slow sips, the coolness grounding me enough to steady myself. The clamor of the city matched the panic inside me. Both refused to settle down. But between the noise and the water sliding down my throat, the truth I'd been avoiding finally broke through: I couldn't keep smiling my way through fear or pretending I was fine. I had to stop thinking my way out of it and start learning how to be with it. That realization, raw as it felt, marked the first tentative step toward healing.

In the months that followed, I opened to the idea that there might be another way to meet my stress—not by fixing it or pushing it away, but by learning to relate to it differently. After all, our habitual reactions to stress are not static—they can soften and shift with practice. In the pause, there is a powerful opening: a space to check in with what's actually happening rather than succumb to the horror stories we keep telling ourselves about it. A space to notice how we're feeling, to sense what our tender hearts need, and to discover the most compassionate way forward.

Mindfulness teaches that self-care is not selfish—it's essential. It teaches that the breath, always available, can be an anchor in any moment of overwhelm. I learned that isolation only deepened my stress, sending danger signals to my nervous system, while connection—even the act of reaching out—reminded me I was safe.

Mindfulness practices showed me I could do hard things without having to do them alone. I no longer saw stress as something to fear or avoid but as a signal: a gentle knock inviting me to go inward and ask, *what do I need right now?* Instead of resisting what was true in the moment, I began meeting it with softness. I began, as Jon Kabat-Zinn often says, to "lay the welcome mat out" to whatever I was feeling—not because it was easy, but because healing couldn't happen until I did.

And soon, life presented an opportunity to see if I could apply some of the mindfulness techniques I was learning

One night, not long after mindfulness became part of my life, I found myself sitting on the kitchen floor, physically and emotionally overwhelmed. Todd was out of town, our basement had flooded, Lindsey was in bed with a stomach bug, and I had slipped on the ice while taking the dogs out and broken my arm. Everything was crumbling. I was crying—exhausted, in pain, and unsure how to manage it all. But instead of falling apart, my default mode, I paused. Instead of spiraling, I remembered my practice. Instead of lamenting, I quieted.

Somewhere between the ache in my chest and the weight of the night, a small part of me whispered: just pause. I closed my eyes and took a few slow, intentional breaths. I tuned into what I could feel—the solid contact of the floor beneath me, the warmth of the air on my skin, and the gentle gurgle of the fish tank. That small pause—a single breath of presence—allowed my body to soften, and I felt a hint of steadiness. I asked myself, *what do I need right now?* The answer was undeniable: *I need more support.*

That evening, I made the decision to find a therapist. It felt like an act of surrender, but also one of strength. I gave myself permission to stop carrying everything alone, to stop protecting everyone else from my struggles, and to let someone hold space for me. This didn't fix my broken arm or clean up the basement, but it helped me stay connected to myself while in the clutches of chaos. It helped me stay open, instead of shutting down. It helped me reach inward, instead of running away. And in that moment, I did the unthinkable: I chose to reach out for support. I was finally willing to admit how much I was struggling—and that I didn't have to carry the burden all on my own.

That revelation didn't change my thinking or beliefs, but it planted a seed. Over time, the combination of therapy and mindfulness helped me to see stress in a different light—not as something to fear, but as something I could approach with care. I began to sense when I was starting to drift, when tension crept into my shoulders, when my breath grew shallow. But instead of pushing through, I paused, I learned to notice, to respond, and to return to a place of balance.

I spent more moments in ease, more moments grounded in peace. Where I once would have worried about how stress might affect my health, I simply acknowledged my feelings and asked, *what do I need right now?* I no longer saw stress as a failure or a threat, but as a messenger. Slowly, I began to trust that I could meet it with compassion instead of dread.

Meeting stress with compassion turned out to be a gentle invitation to notice something deeper: the way my body had been speaking to me all along. Mindfulness helped me tune in to the subtle signals my body consistently sent. I noticed when my muscles were tight, when my jaw was clenched, when I was holding my breath without realizing it. That awareness gave me the power to shift—to exhale, to unwind, to come home to myself.

As I continued to practice mindfulness techniques, I began to release the long-held belief that my self-worth was tied to productivity. I saw how my constant need to accomplish, to perform, and to prove was yet another face of perfectionism. Gradually, I started to let go. I gave myself permission to rest. To pause. To allow. To simply be. And in doing so, I discovered another kind of strength—one rooted not in doing, but in the gentle power of allowing myself to simply exist as I am.

Pause and Reflect

- What does stress feel like in your body? Are there specific places you tend to hold tension?

- What happens when you pause, even for a single breath, in the middle of stress?

- Is there a small act of care or healing you can offer yourself today?

- What stories do you tend to tell yourself when you feel overwhelmed? Are they true?

- How do you usually respond to stress? Is there a response you're beginning to outgrow?

- Can you recall a time you chose rest instead of pushing through? What did that feel like?

- What might it look like to meet your stress with compassion instead of criticism?

- In what ways do perfectionism or people-pleasing show up when you are under stress?

- What does "permission to pause" mean to you right now?

Part Three:
Listening to the Body's Messages

8

Food, Fear, and Finding Balance

"Owning our story and loving ourselves through that process is the bravest thing we'll ever do." — Brené Brown

I do not recall when food stopped feeling safe, only that fear started sitting at the table with me long before MS arrived. By sixteen, I learned that being thin made me more acceptable and easier to love. Every bite held the promise of control or the threat of losing it.

Food was never just fuel for me. It was comfort versus control, and fear versus freedom, all woven together. Living with MS only magnified my fragile relationship with food. For much of my life, food was tangled up with fear—of losing control, of getting sick, of not being enough.

In the world I grew up in, thinness was praised, restriction admired, and discipline mistaken for wellness. After my MS diagnosis, that old conditioning found a new place to flourish. I threw myself into every anti-inflammatory diet protocol promising the possibility of fewer relapses, fewer lesions, fewer unknowns. But the more rigidly I followed the rules, the more disconnected I became from joy, from nourishment, from myself.

When I was sixteen, I was hospitalized with a severe case of mononucleosis. I missed our family trip to the Bahamas and spent days in a hospital bed hooked up to IV steroids to calm my inflamed throat. What a spectacle I was to the resident doctors who stopped by to examine my enormous, angry tonsils.

I lost a considerable amount of weight during my hospital stay, and when I finally returned to school, the reaction I received was unsettling. It was as if I had stepped into a different life overnight. My peers, even some faculty, greeted me with wide eyes and compliments: *"Oh my God, you look SO good—you're so skinny,"* and *"Wow, you could be a model now."* I had never thought of myself as heavy before, or as someone whose body needed fixing, so the praise felt disorienting, even wrong. Inside, I still felt weak and unwell, but suddenly the world was telling me I looked better this way. That surprising reaction from others blurred the lines between sickness and beauty. They called it skinny. What I carried forward was the unspoken belief that being smaller somehow made me more worthy—a belief that stayed with me long after the illness passed.

Certain moments from adolescence remain fixed in our minds. One stands out clearly for me. I walked into the school bathroom, feeling the plain tile floors firm beneath my thin-soled, Mary Jane flats. The smell of cleaning products hung in the air. The hallway noise muffled as the door swung shut behind me like a vault, sealing me inside. In that small, closed in space, I stood in front of the mirror and noticed how my plaid uniform now slid easily around my narrower waist. A powerful thought clicked into place, affirming that this smaller version of me was the one most worthy of being loved. I didn't know how much of my life would be shaped by that thought, how many years I would spend trying to be smaller in many ways long before illness gave me new reasons to fight my body.

I learned early on that my body wasn't just mine—it was up for praise, judgment, or criticism from others. The pressure to stay small took root. It took getting ill to the point of being hospitalized, my throat so swollen I could barely swallow, to reach this diminished size. How was I supposed to maintain it now that I was well? That fear led to the creation of odd, restrictive rituals around food, believing they were the only way to stay slim. At a time when low-fat diets were praised as the pinnacle of health, I not only took the message "smaller is healthier" to heart—I took it to the extreme.

I checked my body at night before bed, making sure I could feel my hip bones and that my stomach felt as flat as it did the night before. These rituals gave me a strange sense of security, as if I could measure my worth with my hands. But it was a slippery slope. The thinner I got, the more I wanted to keep losing weight. It seemed as though it was never enough. No size could ever satisfy me.

What I couldn't see at the time was that the real problem was not the size of my body—it was that I did not feel like enough. At a time when normal teenage challenges made life feel out of control, having a slim physique and winning the admiration of others gave me a false sense of power. I clung to it, even as it chipped away at my peace.

At one point the following year, I started to relax the rules a little— trying to eat with a bit more freedom, and I gained back a few pounds. It felt like progress, but it was fragile. I still measured my worth in pounds and inches, and any slip in the wrong direction felt like a threat.

One summer evening, I stepped into a Blockbuster video store, rows of blue and white VHS cases stretching out in every direction. The smell of candy and buttered popcorn hung in the air as shoppers wove in and out of the aisles around me. And then I saw them—some girls from my school, impossibly slender and seemingly effortless in their smallness. Their long, glossy hair further amplified the contrast between us. I had cut my hair short that year, and suddenly I saw myself through a warped, unkind lens. In an instant, a switch flipped in my mind like it did in the school bathroom the year before. A quiet, emphatic voice insisted I lose more weight and return to the rigid rules in order to be worthy. And with that, the cycle started again, bringing with it the familiar, fleeting sense of safety and control.

I finally exhaled when I went off to college. Maybe it was due to being away from home for the first time, but food wasn't as much something to fear or control. It was no longer a carefully curated list of "safe" options. I let myself eat without worrying about gaining weight or keeping track of all the rules and restrictions that dominated my life for so long.

One night I found myself sitting cross-legged on the dorm room floor with new friends, a greasy Domino's pizza box splayed out between us, our cheek-aching laughter spilling into the hallway. In that moment, food wasn't about rules or restraint, it was about warm, human connection. Sharing that late-night pizza made me feel part of something bigger than myself. For the first time in years, it felt safe to release the rules.

That night, I caught a glimpse of what I would spend years learning through mindfulness and therapy: healing does not occur in isolation. Safety, both with food and within myself, often begins in the presence of others. When I came home after freshman year, that new-found safety and freedom collided with a different kind of welcome. No one asked about the classes I loved, the friends I had made, or the ways I had grown as a person. What I heard instead, directly or between the lines, was that I'd gained weight and that thinner was still better.

That message landed hard, settling in on my very first morning back. Standing in front of the refrigerator, hunger gnawing, I poured a glass of orange juice instead of eating, already sensing the familiar pressure to make myself smaller. My mother's voice floated in from behind me—casual, offhand, the kind of comment I now understand she had probably heard her whole life. "You know orange juice has calories too."

And something in me tightened. I remember thinking, *I can't even drink now.*

And so, I began restricting again. The message that shrinking won approval would echo over and over in the years to come, sometimes delivered by illness itself. Sadly, no one reassured me that it was okay to take up space in the world, just as I was.

Over time, the strain began to show in my body and my immune system weakened. After years of recurring infections and repeated rounds of antibiotics—from the hospital stay in high school and continuing through college—my doctor finally said enough was enough. He insisted that my tonsils had to come out. My mom had been too fearful to agree to the procedure over the years, haunted by the memory of losing her sister during an operation years earlier. But this time, the doctor cautioned that it was negligent to keep waiting. Desperate for relief and worn down from repeated infections, I practically begged her to let me have the surgery.

Not long after the tonsillectomy, the weight I put on in college simply melted. And just like before, the compliments flooded in. Smiles, approving nods, words of praise—as if my shrinking body was a triumph instead of a side effect of being sick and having surgery. The feedback I received carved another lesson deep inside me: *approval comes easily when there is less of me, even if illness is the reason I disappear.*

Little by little, I stopped questioning it. The world kept teaching me the same thing, and I started believing it. It seemed the thinner I got, the more praise I received. Compliments followed me everywhere, reinforcing the belief that being small was not just better—it was admired, even envied. People would say, "You're so lucky. I wish I could look like you. How do you stay so thin?" And slowly, the message seeped in: maybe being tall and thin was the best, most interesting, and lovable part of me.

I never admitted to myself that I had a problem. For years, I told people I was lucky, blessed with a good metabolism—and on some level, I believed it. But beneath that story was the constant calculation of living within a narrow five-pound window. My safety and worth depended on it. If I exceeded the limit, my mom's uneasiness surfaced in subtle, well-meaning comments. If I dipped below it, my dad's worry appeared—once urging me onto a scale, his voice tight as he said, "We will not have a daughter with an eating disorder." I know that both of them loved me deeply; they were responding from their own fears and the beliefs they had been shaped by. But what I absorbed in those moments wasn't concern for my well-being. It was the idea that my body—and how others might see it—carried meaning beyond me.

So, I kept myself in that restricted, fragile middle ground, believing it kept me safe. Safe from judgment. Safe from disapproval. Safe enough to be loved. I learned to hover in that narrow space—never too much, never too little. I did not realize I was teaching myself that love had conditions, and one of them required I take up less space. Little by little, the narrow five-pound range shifted. It moved lower and lower, like a finish line always out of reach, pulling me into more dangerous territory.

My body was paying the price. I had no idea that skipping meals and calling it willpower was stripping my bones of density, throwing my hormones out of balance, and keeping my blood sugar and blood pressure frighteningly low. None of this showed on the outside, but inside, my body was screaming for help. Still, I clung to the rules, rules that kept me safe, lovable, and earning the approval I craved.

For years, my life revolved around staying small, invisible even to myself. But love has a way of making you want more out of life, more connection, more meaning. When Todd and I began to dream of a family, I dared to hope that love and belonging didn't have to depend on how little space I allowed myself to take up—that maybe my life could expand in ways my body was never allowed to.

When Carly was born, healthy and beautiful, I thought I had turned a corner. But soon after, the old need to shrink returned with force. Restricting evolved into a private obsession, and the weight fell off quickly. When we learned, six months later, that I was pregnant again, I experienced a tidal wave of emotions—fear, excitement, and overwhelm all at once. I knew I hadn't been taking care of myself, and guilt swept in almost immediately. I wanted this baby, but I felt anxious, unprepared, and unsure of my body's ability to carry another pregnancy so soon.

My doctor warned that my weight was too low and my body too weak to sustain a pregnancy. I tried everything he prescribed, gulping down Boost drinks with all the hope I had for the tiny life inside me—but it wasn't enough. At three months, I miscarried. Alongside the heartbreak was an unspeakable truth: part of me felt it was for the best, that maybe I wasn't ready yet. And layered beneath it all was the guilt—the belief that I had somehow caused this by not being healthy enough, by not taking care of myself the way a "good mother" would—the way I believed I should.

This was one of many moments in my life where conflicting feelings lived side by side—grief and relief, love and fear, guilt and longing. Eventually, mindfulness taught me how to hold emotions like these with tenderness instead of shame. But at the time, all I knew to do was bury my feelings and keep going.

A couple of years later, I got pregnant again. I nourished my body and my baby with all the care I could muster, and Lindsey arrived healthy and thriving. But once the pregnancy ended, that fragile permission to eat faded away. The cycle of rules and restrictions tightened its grip, pulling me back into a life measured by how little space I deserved to take up.

Motherhood in those early years was full and busy, every day a swirl of playdates, errands, and endless moments I tried to make picture-perfect. My mom had a gift for adding beauty to the simplest things, and she was always ready to help—teaching me how to decorate, plan the most thoughtful birthday parties, and make a house feel warm and welcoming. Her support was a blessing, even as I carried the subtle strain of chasing the image I thought I had to live up to.

Behind the scenes, the effort required to maintain that image wore me down. Losing my eyesight years earlier had marked the beginning of a long season of uncertainty about my body. It would be years before MS was formally diagnosed, along with the agonizing worry it brought about what the future might hold. In the face of so many unknowns, I needed something I could control—and food was the one thing that helped me regain a sense of power over my circumstances.

'Desperate for control, I devoured dietary information, hoping it might keep me safe—safe from relapse, from uncertainty, from the fear I couldn't quiet. I could not foresee that strict nutritional guidelines, initially embraced in the name of healing, would subtly pull me back into old, dangerous patterns. As a perfectionist, I wanted to follow every recommendation flawlessly. I believed doing everything "right" could protect me from future relapses. But old, ingrained patterns of restriction emerged—discipline disguised as dedication.

If you had asked me if I had an eating disorder, I would have been shocked and insisted I did not. Looking back now, I can see I had a serious problem, one that thrived in the years that followed. The truth is, MS gave my harmful patterns the perfect cover. Every new rule, every restriction, could be explained away as a choice to protect my health. I could grow thinner and it was met with praise rather than concern.

When I first discovered a highly structured dietary approach designed to reduce inflammation and support healing, it felt full of promise—a way to fight back, maybe even change the course of my MS. It was grounded in compelling science and often shared through powerful recovery stories that suggested what might be possible. I was desperate to prevent more relapses, more losses, more fear. If this approach had helped others reclaim their bodies, couldn't it do the same for me?

Following the guidelines felt, at least initially, like an act of empowerment—not restriction. The part of me that loved structure and prided herself on doing things "right" was determined to follow every rule. But while I became very good at eliminating what I was told to avoid, I quietly neglected much of what was meant to restore and nourish. Preparing the full, nutrient-rich meals the approach called for felt overwhelming, leaving me unsteady and unsure.

My meals became narrow and predictable, guided more by habit and fear than by nourishment. I told myself I was doing everything I could for my health. But that way of eating felt safe—not because it was nourishing, but because it was familiar, controlled, and easy to manage. In a body already overwhelmed, restriction came naturally. Nourishment did not.

What I didn't yet understand was that approaches designed to heal can land very differently in bodies shaped by fear, perfectionism, and a history of disordered eating.

After years of trying to control my health through rigid rules and restriction, my body began to unravel. I developed Hashimoto's, an autoimmune thyroid condition. I went through menopause in my early forties. My bone density slid from osteopenia to osteoporosis by my fifties. My blood pressure dipped dangerously low; my blood sugar levels swung wildly, forcing me to wear a glucose monitor after several terrifying episodes sent me to the hospital. The panic attacks I thought were behind me returned without warning. My blood chemistry labs were all over the place. My hair came out in clumps, my skin cracked with dryness, and my nails grew brittle. I looked frail and gaunt. Anxious and unstable in my own body, I felt weaker and more vulnerable than ever.

Eventually, my blood pressure and heart rate became so erratic that I was hospitalized and diagnosed with Hyperadrenergic POTS—an imbalance of the autonomic nervous system. Terrified, I recall thinking this was worse than anything MS had thrown at me. And through it all, no one ever questioned my weight. At doctor's appointments, I heard things like "nice and low" when they weighed me, or "you're nice and thin" spoken almost as praise. Not one person asked about my diet or my troubled history with food. I was getting away with living by the rules, and it was killing me.

I got so tired of feeling exhausted and fragile that I slowly woke up to the painful truth: I was not eating to support my health or MS at all. My choices were about fear, control, and old wounds I had not faced. That realization broke something wide open in me. It was excruciating, but it was the first brave step toward facing the fear that ruled my relationship with food—and toward finding true healing.

This marked the beginning of seeing my struggles with food and body image through a different lens. I knew I had to do the inner work necessary to heal my relationship with both. I acknowledged that it had never really been about the food or the number on the scale. It had always been about safety. About control. About trying to soothe or tame a fear that extended well beyond the food on my plate.

I found a knowledgeable dietitian who worked with people struggling with eating disorders. After sending her my most recent blood labs and filling out intake paperwork, I set an appointment to meet her in person. She looked at me—not with judgment, but with genuine concern, and said matter-of-factly, "You are mal-nourished." It was a wake-up call. Deep down, I already knew it, but hearing those words spoken by a professional, sparked a shift I was too afraid to make on my own.

I felt a deep sadness as I told her my challenges with food began when I was only sixteen—and here I was, in my mid-fifties, fighting the same battle. But this time, I was ready to make peace with food and with my body. With her support, I began the hard work of nourishing myself and restoring the weight my body needed to be healthy.

Letting go of the countless food rules I had clung to for decades was far from easy. I wasn't only afraid of what might happen to my body, but those rigid rules had become proof—to myself and to others—that I was doing everything I could to stay healthy. They were my armor, my illusion of control. Releasing them meant admitting to and grieving for all the years fear had stolen from me. I began to sense a small opening—one that asked me to choose myself.

That is when the real work began. I leaned on my mindfulness practice to begin turning inward, asking myself the difficult ques-tions and truly listening to the answers. It was the hard, uncom-fortable work of trying to understand what my body needed—to restore weight, lift the mental fog, and feel free, safe, and able to enjoy food again.

It wasn't simple. Living with multiple autoimmune conditions—MS, Hashimoto's, and POTS—meant my body was facing unique challenges, and I still needed to consider which foods might fuel inflammation and which might calm it. All the while, I was trying to heal my relationship with food and loosen the grip of restriction. It was messy and complicated, and although there is still work to be done, I am slowly learning to trust and nourish my body.

Mindfulness reminds me I do not have to do this perfectly. I can make mistakes. I can change course if needed. I can speak my truth instead of keeping it buried in shame and secrecy. And perhaps most importantly, I can trust others to help me and lean on the support that was right in front of me instead of carrying this burden alone.

Even knowing this, I was nervous to tell Todd I needed support—afraid of the financial cost of seeing specialists, ashamed of needing help for something like this so late in life, and guilt-ridden for adding one more health challenge to what he had already carried alongside me for years. When I finally shared my struggles with him, his response was one of love and compassion. I could see in his eyes that he genuinely wanted me to get the help I needed and that he would stand beside me. In that moment, the relief, the closeness, and the sense of shared burden reminded me just how healing it is to know you are not alone. Whenever I felt alone, my body stayed on high alert, flooded with anxiety. When I let others in—when I felt supported, understood, connected—my breath came easier and my body began to trust again. Connection, I was learning, was every bit as nourishing as the food on my plate.

With the guidance of my incredibly supportive dietician and the intensive work I did with my therapist, I made significant progress on healing my relationship with food and my body. It was not a straight line. There were setbacks, and I've since learned they are more the norm than the exception. Each setback, much like every MS relapse, taught me more about resilience and what it means to keep showing up for myself.

Mindfulness will always need to be part of my journey. This is especially true during times of heightened stress, when old patterns whisper their way back in. I have to stay vigilant and awake to myself. So, now I pause, breathe, ask what is going on beneath the superficial urge to control or restrict. I've learned to reach out to others to ensure I am not carrying it alone, and to offer myself the same compassion I extend to others. Healing, I have discovered, is not about never slipping. It is about finding my way back—to my body, my breath, my own heart—each time I drift away. Every mindful breath is a reminder that healing is not a destination but a homecoming.

In time, I began to feel safe in my own body—not because I had physically perfected it, but because I had finally begun to trust it. That trust gave me the strength to stay in the process, even when it felt emotionally uncomfortable to restore my weight. No matter how uncomfortable, I continued to trust the process, staying committed to choices that supported both my recovery and my health. I wasn't perfect, but I tried to meet myself with compassion—especially when I slipped or made choices that did not support my healing.

One habit I had to examine was my tendency to rely on famil-iar, "safe" choices instead of fully nourishing myself. While those habits once served a purpose, they could quietly pull me back into old patterns of avoidance and restriction—especially when I was tired or overwhelmed.

On days when I defaulted to what felt easiest, I didn't punish myself. I got curious. I asked: *What am I really needing right now? Is there another way to meet that need?* Meeting myself with compassion allowed me to gently change course, again and again, choosing nourishment over fear.

Applying mindfulness to my recovery allowed me to meet my-self where I was without judgment. Over time, I noticed real shifts: my stomach was no longer constantly bloated, I was sleeping bet-ter, and my anxiety was fading. My thinking grew clearer, I felt more joy and ease, and my relationship with food softened.

With that fear quieted, I heard a voice from deep within my body guiding me toward what it truly needed. I came to accept that approaches that worked well for others were not working for me, and that my path to healing might look different. I began using my mindfulness practice to turn inward and reconnect with my body. I no longer needed someone else's rules or protocols—I could listen inwardly, discover what nourished me, and trust that inner guidance. Looking back, my body had been speaking to me all along, but it wasn't until I slowed down and tuned in that I could understand what it was trying to say.

The more I nourished myself, the healthier I got. One day, as I logged in to review my lab work, I scrolled through the results and could not find a single blood parameter out of range—something I hadn't seen in years. It took a few moments to sink in: *everything is within range.* What a rush of relief, accomplishment, and gratitude.

Not long after, I noticed the changes showing up in quieter ways. My blood pressure stabilized and no longer ran dangerously low. My bone density improved, reversing from osteoporosis to osteopenia. My POTS symptoms faded. My blood sugar stabilized. Fewer, smaller clumps of hair clogged the shower drain. My nails stopped splitting. My skin looked brighter. People were noticing—not my size, but my health. Instead, I heard, "You look so healthy," a confirmation that my body was healing—and that I was learning how to support it.

For years, obsessive thoughts about food kept me pulled out of the present moment. Even as I practiced mindfulness, I was unknowingly creating strain through the very habits I believed were keeping me safe. As I nourished myself and healed, I began to see that it wasn't only my relationship with food that was changing—it was my relationship with life.

I've come to understand that healing does not follow a single path. What supports one person may not support another, because we all carry different histories, bodies, and needs. I've had relapses both on and off medication, while following and stepping away from structured approaches. For me, healing has come from honoring what works for my own body and allowing myself the flexibility to change course.

There is freedom in not needing everyone else to understand or agree with my decisions. That is not to say I don't feel the pull of wanting the approval of others, but I no longer depend on it. I can listen to suggestions, weigh opinions, and then go inward and ask myself what feels best for me in that moment. No decision has to be final—I can change my mind, try something new, pivot. I can live with the knowledge that others might choose differently, and I can still trust myself.

That self-trust mattered more than I realized, because stress has always been my biggest trigger—both for MS flares as well as struggles with my physical and mental health. Mindfulness has helped me notice what I need most and to respond with care, instead of control. Now I tune in and ask: *What does my body, my nervous system, need to feel safe in this moment?* And if that answer happens to change, it is okay.

Before I learned to trust my own experience, I felt guilty every time my MS symptoms flared. Even when I was doing everything I had been told was "right"—following structured approaches and taking prescribed medication—I still had relapses, often after periods of significant stress. I interpreted each flare as a personal failure, proof that I hadn't managed my life or my emotions well enough. What a terrible weight to carry.

I've come to believe that one of the dangers of any approach that promises control over a disease is the shame it can leave behind when symptoms return. Did my relapses really mean I had failed? Or was my body signaling that I needed more support, more rest, and a different relationship with stress? What I began to see was this: when stress went unmanaged, both my health and my quality of life suffered.

At the heart of my journey with food, fear, and finding balance are three intertwined lessons: releasing the old belief that my worth depends on body size, softening the chronic fear and anxiety that fed my illness, and embracing a gentler, more compassionate way forward. These are not milestones to be reached but practices to be lived—guiding me back, again and again, to balance, to trust, and to a sense of belonging within myself—one mindful moment at a time.

Pause and Reflect

- When you reflect on your own relationship with food, what messages, spoken or unspoken, have shaped your beliefs about nourishment, control, or body image?

- Have you ever used food (or restriction) as a way to feel safe, in control, or "good enough"? What was happening in your life at the time?

- What does *balance* mean to you—not just around food, but in your relationship with your body and your emotions?

- Can you recall a time when you began to listen to your body with more compassion or curiosity?

- If your body could speak to you right now, what might it be asking for?

9

HONORING MY ENERGY

"No one can tell you what your track will be or how to know what calls you and brings you to life. That's your work to do."— Boyd Varty

Some days, my body feels tired long before my mind is ready to admit it. Fatigue doesn't always leave a mark you can see. Sometimes it is obvious, written in slumped shoulders or heavy eyes. But often it hides beneath the surface—quiet, invisible, and profoundly shaping how we move through the world.

Some truths live in the body long before we learn how to name them.

You don't have to have a chronic illness to understand what it feels like to be exhausted and still feel pressured to show up, smile, and say yes. But when that pressure becomes your norm, the ability to hear your body's whispers, to honor your limits without shame, and to trust your inner knowing slips away.

Of all the symptoms I have lived with, fatigue has been the hardest to explain—and the one that taught me the most about honoring my energy. Not the kind of tiredness that sleep fixes, but the kind that makes it overwhelming to have the television on while someone is talking to me—when I can be in a room with people I love, feeling grateful and happy, and still be so exhausted

I could cry. The kind that leaves me wanting to participate, to attend, to say yes, and still knowing in my body that it is simply impossible.

It never occurred to me that strength could mean resting or saying no. I had internalized the idea that being strong meant pushing through, saying yes, and doing more. It wasn't that I lost the ability to listen to my body; I had never been taught how to listen to it. It wasn't modeled for me. I didn't even realize it was missing.

Living with MS—and later, discovering mindfulness—taught me another way. I began to unlearn the pressure to prove and perform. Slowly, I gained the power to say no, to choose rest without guilt, and to care for myself without apology.

These lessons didn't come easily. They arrived through hard moments, quiet grief, and years of trial and error. I remember pausing one afternoon, noticing the familiar pull to push through, and choosing instead to sit, breathe, and listen. It was a small moment, but something shifted. Each time I honored my energy, I grew more rooted in self-trust.

I learned that honoring my energy isn't a sign of laziness or weakness. It is the wisdom my body had been trying to teach me all along—one boundary, one breath, one brave "no" at a time.

As I began to listen more closely, I started to understand what fatigue was really asking of me.

Fatigue is like carrying an invisible weight—one that slows my body, clouds my mind, and makes even the simplest tasks feel overwhelming. It can make it hard to eat when I'm starving. Sometimes the fatigue is so intense that I struggle to speak—the words are there, but forming them feels impossible. A trip to the grocery store can be more taxing than running a marathon—which, iron-ically, I later did.

And fatigue can be deeply lonely. It forces you to say no to things you desperately want to say yes to. It can leave you sitting alone in a dark, quiet room because the noise and light of everyday life are simply too much. In that stillness—sad, confused, overstimu-lated—you may find yourself crying without knowing why. The smallest things can suddenly feel crushing.

There is a particular kind of grief in watching the world move on while your body demands that you pause. It took time for me to understand that fatigue would become part of life with MS. At first, it was easy to explain away my exhaustion—to blame a restless night or a packed schedule. But this depletion was differ-ent. It didn't lift with rest or resolve with time. Instead, it asked something harder of me: to let go of the illusion that I could keep going as I always had. My body was no longer willing to play along.

As I learned to live with the invisible weight of fatigue, certain memories etched themselves into my understanding of this new normal. One of the clearest came about a year after my first major relapse—the one that took my vision—as we were headed into New York City to see *The Nutcracker*. My daughters Carly and Lindsey, still so little then, my mom, my sister-in-law, her mom, and I all gathered to carry on a tradition I have treasured since childhood. Spending the day with three generations of women was especially meaningful, and I was excited to share it with my girls. We even rented a limo to make the day feel special—a small luxury meant to add joy and ease. But while everything around me looked celebratory, I was inexplicably drained.

I had terrible neck and back pain, a splitting headache, and a profound exhaustion. It made it incredibly difficult to stay present in an experience I so wanted to savor. I sank into the velvet seat of the theater, trying to hide how off I felt. When the curtain rose, I thought: *What is this? Why do I feel like this?* There was no visible cause. I was wrapped in warmth and tradition, surrounded by joy, yet I struggled to stay upright in a world suddenly too bright, too loud, and too crowded. I didn't have language for it then, but I knew something in my body had shifted.

Over time, my fatigue carried an edge of fear, hinting at a deeper problem I could not ignore. It wasn't only tiredness—it was a force that pressed harder the more I tried to push it aside. After several experiences like the Nutcracker night, I recognized the true cost of pushing through. My body begins to shut down. I get shaky, dizzy, flooded with stimuli. My nervous system goes into overwhelm, and even turning my head makes the room spin. Waves of anxiety follow, tipping me into panic. It's as if my whole system overheats and short circuits all at once. I want to be present, but I become unreachable—even to myself.

For a long time, I over-explained. I apologized whenever fatigue showed up. I was desperate for people to understand because a part of me longed for someone to say it was okay to rest. I was still seeking external permission. If I could get you to see why I wasn't participating, I could feel relief. But if I couldn't, it added another layer of stress.

If I failed to gain your understanding, I would push through—trying to meet expectations instead of honoring what I truly needed. Saying "no" felt impossible unless I could justify it with proof. And because deep, cellular fatigue is invisible, I often felt unseen—as if my needs were not real unless someone else agreed.

Learning to trust my intuition over the opinions of others has been one of the hardest—and most healing—parts of this journey. It is a shift that has taken time and has been tested again and again in real-life moments. Moments like traveling back East to visit friends and family after our move to Arizona. These summer trips took an enormous toll on my body, and I often relapsed or flared after coming home. The emotional labor, crowded schedule, overstimulation, and constant pull to fit everyone in became too much.

Eventually, the cost grew too high, and I had to stop overriding what my body was asking of me. That choice was painful. It left some people hurt or confused, and it took me a long time to release the guilt that followed. I can also see now that I didn't always know how to communicate my limits clearly. I assumed people would understand—or that if they didn't ask, it meant they didn't care. In truth, I hadn't yet learned how to name what I needed or trust that it was okay to ask for it.

Over time, I came to understand that relationships are meant to be mutual. If maintaining one requires me to carry all the weight—to initiate, to travel, to explain, to absorb misunderstandings—then something essential is missing. Love isn't always enough to sustain a relationship; it also takes effort, understanding, and reciprocity.

Releasing the pressure to make myself go—even when I wanted to, even when it disappointed others—was one of the first ways I learned to truly honor my limits. It didn't mean I cared less or wanted connection any less. It meant I was finally willing to stop sacrificing my well-being to prove it. That lesson returned again and again—sometimes quietly, in small choices, and sometimes in ways that were far more personal and painful.

Some of the most painful choices are the ones where love and limits collide. For me, one of those moments came when I made the decision not to attend my nephew's wedding. I knew it would be painful, and it was. It devastated my brother—and I understand now that the impact likely reached beyond him.

The decision itself was clear, but it was anything but easy. I was not physically or emotionally up to making the trip, especially with the strain of complicated family dynamics that were going on at the time. I knew the choice was the right one for my health, yet it was deeply painful to know it would hurt people I love—and harder still to realize that my reasons were not fully understood.

I tried, in the ways I knew how at the time, to help my brother understand. He even ordered a book about MS. Later, I sent him a podcast I had recorded, hoping that hearing me speak about living with MS might offer a window into what my days actually feel like. But we never spoke about it, and that silence left a void.

These are the moments that ache—not because the choice is wrong, but because it is hard. Mindfulness has taught me to meet these moments with compassion for everyone involved, including myself, and not punish myself with guilt. The ache doesn't mean we've chosen wrongly; it means we are human—learning, loving, and doing the best we can. One of the kindest things we can do for another is try to understand pain we cannot see. Even the smallest effort to listen can be a form of care.

Moments like that helped me understand how easily invisible struggles can be misunderstood. That is why comments like "But you look so good" can land with a sting. They may be meant kindly, but they can feel dismissive, as if pain, fatigue, and daily challenges don't count unless they are visible. When there is no outward sign of the incredible energy it takes to get through the day, other people's understanding can fade.

We all carry things others can't see: illness, fatigue, anxiety, depression, and loneliness to name a few. When we are struggling, what we often long for most is to feel seen, to be asked how we are really doing, and to know that someone cares enough to want to know. I have felt the frustration of having my own struggles overlooked—not out of indifference, but simply because they are invisible. And it hurts.

At times, I wished my symptoms were more visible—not for pity, but for understanding. The symptoms that affect me most—fatigue, numbness, blurred vision, and cognitive fog—don't show up in photos. They don't invite questions or concern. When you appear fine on the outside, people assume you are. And when you're not, the gap between how you feel and how you are perceived can be vast. Mindfulness has taught me that even in that gap, I can meet myself with care.

When others don't understand what you are going through, it's easy to feel like you're letting them down—for needing rest, for saying no, for not showing up. But most of the time, you're simply trying to keep going. Through mindfulness, I've come to see that I don't need everyone to understand. I can release the urge to over-explain or apologize. Those who remain—the people who truly listen and accept me as I am—are the ones whose relationships I cherish most.

It is interesting to see the different ways people show up in our lives, each offering something unique and meaningful. Some friends bring laughter or share a love of adventure while others offer simple, grounding moments—quiet conversations, shared walks, or a comforting presence. It's not about expecting one relationship to be everything—but honoring the ones that meet us where we are.

For me, honoring those relationships has meant being honest about my limits, even when it means saying no to things I long to do. There was a time when I felt the weight of every invitation I declined. Large gatherings, lively parties, and community events are things I love—but with a nervous system that tires easily and flares unpredictably, they often come with a cost. In those settings, the effort it takes to stay present—to process noise, movement, and conversation while masking how I'm really feeling—can leave me depleted for days.

Learning to honor my energy doesn't mean closing the door on everything I love. It means choosing with care—making space for what lights me up while tending to what keeps me well. Sometimes, the honest answer leads me to stay home. Other times, when the occasion holds deep meaning, I choose to rally.

There are still occasions I choose to show up for, even knowing the cost. When something holds deep meaning, I prepare carefully—clearing space before and after, listening to my body, and making sure I have room to recover. That rhythm of preparation and rest has become essential to how I live, love, and participate in what matters most.

And nowhere was that lesson tested more profoundly than in motherhood.

There were nights I cried to my husband, convinced I was failing as a mother. But with his understanding and the help of a wise and compassionate therapist, I began to see things differently. By saying no, by setting boundaries, by giving myself permission to rest, I wasn't letting my daughters down. I was modeling how to honor their own needs with compassion. I wasn't showing them a mother who had it all together. I was showing them a woman who listened to her body, honored her limits, and said no when she needed to. And that, I believe, is a lasting lesson to pass on.

There were moments when the cost of showing up weighed heavily. I remember my daughters asking, with honest curiosity, why I didn't go out more or have more friends. Their questions stirred an old sense of inadequacy, until I began to understand that what they really needed wasn't more from me—it was a mother who was true to herself.

I used to compare myself to other moms—the ones who could welcome a house full of kids for playdates without stress, sign up for every volunteer role at school, and never run out of energy. My nervous system is uniquely wired. My threshold is lower. Honoring that has required courage—and a deepening sense of self-compassion.

The people I let close—my husband, my daughters, the friends, and family members who know my heart—don't ask me to be more. They love me as I am. And maybe that's what I have been teaching my daughters all along: that our worth isn't measured by how much we do, but by how fully we love; that presence matters more than perfection; and that being loved for who we are—not for what we achieve—is one of life's greatest gifts.

Honoring my energy as a mother taught me to say no with compassion, protect my reserves, and choose presence over perfection. That same wisdom also led me to expansion. Honoring my energy doesn't always mean doing less or pulling back. Sometimes it means saying yes to what truly matters—letting my energy guide me forward in ways that honor my truth and well-being.

Listening to my energy didn't always mean pulling back. Sometimes, it invited me to move toward something that mattered deeply.

After living with MS for nearly five years, I decided to run a half marathon—not to prove anything to anyone, but to reconnect with myself. To rebuild trust in my body. I approached it gently, pacing myself with intention and listening closely to what I needed along the way.

I had never been a runner. But while visiting my brother, I noticed a training book on the kitchen counter and felt a quiet spark of possibility. I followed a structured plan—something that felt grounding and safe—and slowly, mile by mile, I surprised myself. Each small gain felt like a miracle.

Running became less about pushing and more about partnership. I wasn't running to escape my illness; I was learning how to move with it. The experience showed me another face of honoring my energy: sometimes it means resting, and sometimes it means rising.

On race day, running through the streets of my hometown felt exhilarating. Cheers lined the sidewalks, and for a while, I felt unstoppable. But in the final miles, my body began to fade. Doubt crept in as my legs grew heavy and my breath shallow.

And then I heard them. *"GO MOMMY!"*

I spotted my daughters, beaming and cheering with everything they had. Their joy filled me with strength I didn't know I still had. I found a final surge and carried it all the way to the finish line.

Crossing that line was a triumph—not just for the miles I ran, but for the resilience it took to get there. In that moment, I proved to myself that I could live with MS and still choose something bold.

And yet, the recovery told another truth. I could barely walk afterward. My legs ached, my energy was gone, and my nervous system felt frayed. The race empowered me—but it also reminded me how tender my limits still were.

After the race, I let myself rest and refuel—body and spirit alike. I listened for what I needed instead of following rules or expectations, honoring the effort I had asked of myself.

That experience taught me something vital about honoring my energy: when I say yes to something physically or emotionally demanding—even when it is meaningful—I have to create space to prepare and time to recover. Skipping either one leaves me depleted, a reminder that strength isn't only about what I take on, but how I care for myself afterward.

The marathon showed me that honoring my energy doesn't mean avoiding challenge. It means tending to myself with intention as I move toward what matters—trusting both my capacity and my limits.

One profound way this lesson has shown up is through our trips to South Africa. The journey itself is demanding—more than twenty hours of travel across three flights, including a long layover in London. It is physically exhausting. And yet, for our family, it has been worth every mile because what awaits on the other end feels like a sacred, spiritual homecoming.

We have been deeply fortunate to return four times, always to the same place: Londolozi, a third-generation, family-run safari camp in the Sabi Sands, part of the Greater Kruger region. I don't take that privilege lightly. We return not because it is easy, but because it nourishes us in a way few places ever have. There is something profound about being in the bush—stepping into a rhythm that invites you to slow down, listen, and soften. The people we have met there—especially the guides and staff—embody mindfulness without ever naming it, fully attuned to the land, to one another, and to the present moment. Their warmth and presence create a quiet settling inside me.

One rainy morning, we set out for a game drive bundled in heavy black ponchos. Beneath the wide canopy of a massive natal mahogany tree, the guides set up coffee. I cupped a warm mug of hot chocolate between my hands, my body waking slowly in the morning chill, when a family of elephants appeared. They moved past us so closely we could hear them breathing, then joined us beneath the same tree, grazing peacefully on the leaves that sheltered us. We quite literally shared breakfast with the elephants. It was one of those rare moments that hush you into silence because words cannot fully contain what you are witnessing.

There is no cell service out in the bush, no constant pull outward. You wake before sunrise for game drives, rest during the heat of the day, and return again at dusk. The pace is slow, intentional, and spacious. In the in-between hours, there is yoga beneath open skies, quiet reflection, and meals shared with people who feel more like family than strangers. The experience heals you while you are there and stays with you long after you leave.

But it is also a trip that asks a great deal of my body. Not all effort costs the body the same way. Nourishment and depletion are not opposites of difficulty. I have learned that what matters most is not how hard something is, but whether it ultimately restores me or drains me. South Africa requires preparation, pacing, and reverence for my limits—but it gives back in equal measure.

I prepare for it the way I would a marathon. I rest in the days leading up to travel. I pack with care, giving myself permission to move slowly. I build in recovery time once we arrive and again when we return home. I say no to certain activities so I can say yes to what matters most: being present with the people I love in a place that reminds me who I am.

That awareness has served me again and again—especially in the journeys that took me far from home and into some of the most meaningful experiences of my life.

MS has shown me that honoring your energy doesn't mean saying no to every hard thing. It means choosing wisely—prioritizing what fills your spirit and creating the support you need to do it well. Some experiences ask a lot, but they also give back in ways that restore and expand me.

Over time, I've learned that honoring my energy isn't only about what I do in the moment, but what I build around those moments. I now pay attention to what drains me and what restores me, and I plan accordingly. I build space before and after demanding experiences so my body knows it will be cared for. That cushion of time sends a powerful message to my nervous system: you are safe.

Not everything is worth the toll. If something will deplete me, I pause. If it will bring meaning, connection, or joy, I prepare. And if I'm considering something for someone else's sake, I ask whether I will be supported if I need to move slowly or step back. When the answer is no, I choose to decline with care.

Honoring my energy isn't about doing everything. It's about choosing what is worth it and honoring myself enough to meet it with intention. MS doesn't mean I can't do hard or beautiful things—it means I must do them in a way that aligns with my spirit. Thoughtfully. Intentionally. And with care.

My mindfulness practice helped me tune into my body, my emotions, and my limits. I learned to stop pushing through pain and listen instead—to pause and ask, *What do I need in this moment?* And slowly, I gave myself permission to honor the answer, even when it meant saying no, disappointing others, or missing out.

When I honor my energy, I release the pressure to do everything. I prioritize what aligns with my values, needs, and well-being. I trust my body's signals—resting before I'm depleted, saying no without shame, and saying yes to what nourishes me rather than what simply looks good to others.

I have come to appreciate that honoring my energy is not a limitation. It is wisdom—quiet, steady, and transformative. It reminds me that presence matters more than perfection, and that caring for myself does not require guilt or apology. Perhaps that is the lesson I carry forward—and the one I hope others may find too: that honoring our energy is not weakness, but guidance—an invitation to come home to ourselves and live in a way that feels authentically our own.

Pause and Reflect

- When do you feel most energized, grounded, or alive? How are you caring for yourself in those moments?

- Can you recall a time when your body or spirit whispered (or shouted) for rest? How did you respond?

- What would it look like to honor your energy more consistently? What would you need to say no to, and what might open up for you if you did?

- In what ways have you been overriding your body's signals? What might shift if you paused and asked, *"What do I need right now?"*

- Think about the activities, people, or environments that fill your cup. Which of these might you choose more intentionally in the future?

10

Coming Home to My Body

"Nothing ever goes away until it has taught us what we need to know." —Pema Chödrön

The body holds wisdom—but it took me years, and more than a few relapses, to learn how to listen to it. Each flare arrived with fear—fear of what I might lose, what might never come back. In the early years, I saw relapses as proof that I was doing something wrong, that no matter how carefully I followed diets, medications, or advice, my body could not be trusted.

Over time, something shifted. I began to notice that relapses didn't arrive randomly. They came with patterns, with signals I was only beginning to recognize. They asked me to slow down, to rest, to pay attention to where I was pushing past my limits. My body—fragile and unpredictable at times—was not betraying me. It was trying to communicate.

I wish I could say this understanding came all at once, but it didn't. It was forged slowly, relapse by relapse, as I stumbled, resisted, and learned. Each one carried its own fear, but also its own lessons—truths that, over time, shaped how I've come to live with MS.

When I think back to relapses before mindfulness became part of my life, one stands out. It was the time I lost my vision—the relapse that eventually drew me to Jon Kabat-Zinn's MBSR course. I've already described it in this book, but what distinguishes it from later relapses is the overwhelming fear that accompanied it. I lived in a near-constant state of anxiety, checking my eyesight repeatedly, desperate for reassurance that my vision was improving. Panic spilled into other parts of my life, shaping how I moved through my days.

I remember gripping the steering wheel, lightheaded as panic set in, blasting the air conditioning and whispering, *You are okay... you are okay*, as I eased into the right lane and focused on my breath. I felt unsafe in my own body—unsteady, unprotected, chasing control that slipped away no matter how tightly I tried to hold on.

With time, mindfulness gave me steadier ground to stand on. The body that once felt frightening and unpredictable began to feel less like something to battle and more like something to listen to. I could meet sensations that once sent me spiraling with greater calm and trust. That quiet shift opened my curiosity to other practices—and eventually led me to Yoga Nidra.

After years of experiencing the restorative rest of Yoga Nidra, I wanted to study it more deeply. Signing up for a teacher training felt like a natural extension of my mindfulness work—an invitation to learn more about a practice that had touched my life in profound ways. I imagined offering Yoga Nidra alongside the meditation and mindfulness classes I was already teaching.

The program was immersive, spanning full weekends from Friday evening through Sunday night. I loved the material, but the long days of sitting, absorbing, and practicing took a toll. By the end of the first weekend, I felt wrung out—exhausted in a way that was familiar but not yet alarming. I told myself I simply needed to be gentle with myself between sessions.

Then something new surfaced. My tongue felt oddly numb and cold. At first, I brushed it off and called my dentist, hoping for a simple explanation. When he urged me to contact my neurologist, a familiar unease settled in. I had grown used to my body doing "weird things," but when the numbness spread to my face, I knew what it meant. I was facing another relapse.

The scans confirmed a new lesion in my brainstem. My neurologist explained that its location required aggressive treatment and outlined my options. Once, this news would have shattered me. Now, I breathed. I stayed present. Instead of fear, I felt a quiet strength rise within me.

I decided to return to a disease-modifying medication for a few years—long enough to stabilize things until the risk of future relapses might lessen. Todd was there, and we talked it through. I asked my doctor what she would recommend if it were her own health. Most of all, I trusted myself, knowing I could revisit the decision if needed. What once would have felt agonizing arrived with clarity—steady and grounded, shaped by years of mindfulness practice.

That clarity also meant saying no to something I deeply wanted: the Yoga Nidra teacher training. I knew continuing would push my body beyond its limits. Letting go was painful, especially because a friend had joined the program to do it alongside me. When she shared how meaningful the training was, I felt both happiness for her and a quiet ache for myself. This wasn't the first delay—a back injury had already postponed it once—and for a moment, old grief surfaced.

But beneath that grief was a steadier voice: *Not now. Rest. Trust that when the time is right, you'll return.* So I stepped back and gave myself permission to wait.

When I returned a year later, I carried more than readiness—I carried the strength the waiting had given me. I felt grounded and whole. What once felt like loss had ripened into a gift, reminding me that disappointment, when met with patience and trust, can become a powerful teacher.

Relapses weren't the only way my body spoke to me. Sometimes its messages came through the choices I made about how I lived in my body—something I came to understand through the story of my breast implants.

After the birth of our two daughters, I was still wrestling with disordered eating and a distorted relationship with my body. I wasn't nourishing myself properly, and after pregnancy and breastfeeding, my chest felt almost nonexistent. I had always been small, but now I felt deeply inadequate.

I remember sitting at a pool one afternoon, looking around and feeling convinced I didn't measure up. I came home in tears, longing for reassurance from my husband that I was loved exactly as I was. Instead, he quickly suggested I get implants. It wasn't what I needed. I was searching for reassurance that I was already enough, and his excitement—so immediate, so revealing—confirmed the fear I hadn't yet learned how to name: that I wasn't enough as I was.

At that time in my life, I hadn't yet done the inner work needed to find my voice. I didn't know how to say, *Your response hurts me. I need to feel loved as I am.* Afraid that honesty might cost me love, I swallowed my discomfort and silenced my needs—a pattern many of us fall into when we don't yet trust our own worth.

In the end, I buried the unease and convinced myself to go along with it. The surgery came and went, but instead of bringing the confidence I had hoped for, it left me with a quiet ache: this wasn't what I wanted.

Living with implants was a daily reminder that I was carrying something that didn't belong to me. I tried to accept them, pushing aside the discomfort of living in a body that no longer felt like my own. Deep down, I knew they weren't the answer. The real struggle—just as it had been with food and body image—was never about size. It was about believing I was enough.

It would take many years, and an unexpected conversation, for that truth to fully come into focus. Twenty years later, while talking with a neighbor on our quiet street, she shared her story of breast implant illness. Strange symptoms—rashes, pain, swelling, fatigue—had haunted her for years until she finally had her implants removed. Almost overnight, her health returned.

As she spoke, goosebumps rose across my skin. *Could this be me too?* I wondered. My first MS relapse had happened just three months after my implant surgery—could they have been part of the story all along?

I rushed inside, opened my laptop, and read story after story. The symptoms were achingly similar. Tears filled my eyes as clarity broke through: it was time to get rid of the implants I had never wanted and come home to the body I had spent years resisting. The decision was both terrifying and liberating—terrifying because it meant facing old insecurities, and liberating because it asked me to accept myself as I was. I realized then that coming home to myself wasn't about changing my body at all. It was about learning to love and trust it.

My friend—who has been like a sister to me since our first day of kindergarten—stayed with me after the surgery. She has loved me through every season of my life, and her presence wrapped me in comfort. Knowing she was also a nurse gave me added reassurance, especially as I navigated the anxiety that often follows medical procedures. Her care was a quiet reminder that we don't have to face hard moments alone.

Because I was more honest about what I needed, I felt supported not only by her, but by Todd and my loved ones as well. Their collective care created the safety I needed to settle into myself again. I began to see beauty where I had once seen only imperfection, recognizing that home was never outside of me—it had always been here, in my body.

Coming home to myself opened the door to a new way of preparing for surgery—anchored in trust instead of fear. Peggy Huddleston's *Prepare for Surgery, Heal Faster* echoed the impact Jon Kabat-Zinn had made decades earlier, like a bookend to my journey. Each night, I listened to her guided meditations, visualizing a smooth surgery and an easy recovery.

I was met with an openness I hadn't experienced in my early MS years. My doctors welcomed my intentions and treated me as a partner in my own healing. For the first time, I felt seen not just as a patient, but as a whole person—affirming what mindfulness had taught me all along: healing begins when mind and body are honored together.

Incredibly, many of those intentions unfolded. I woke up calm and clear, never needed pain medication, and recovered more easily than I expected. Walking into surgery on my own, I felt grounded and steady. Mindfulness had become something I could rely on.

When the implants came out, I felt a deep sense of relief and alignment—as though my body and I were finally on the same side. My husband's apology for encouraging me to get them years earlier added another layer of healing. Looking back, I can see that my body was never working against me. It was trying, in its own way, to be heard.

I can't say for certain whether the implants contributed to my health issues, or whether removing them changed the course of my MS. What I can say is that I felt lighter and freer without them. Today, I can look at my small chest—affectionately nicknamed my "itty bitty's"—and smile. At a recent dress fitting, the seamstress noted the difference between my top and bottom measurements. Instead of shame, I felt gratitude. This is me—nourished and whole. It isn't about changing my body; it's about loving and appreciating it for what it does, exactly as it is.

I don't share this story to suggest that implants are wrong for everyone. I know many women who have them and love them. They simply were never the answer for me. What I was really longing for was to learn how to love myself and trust that I was already enough. Removing the implants marked the beginning of that homecoming, and for that, I am grateful.

I will never welcome relapses, but I no longer fear them. They remind me of the limits of control, but also of the possibility of renewal. They ask me to pause, soften, and return to what matters most.

Setbacks aren't unique to MS. We all face seasons when our lives fall apart in ways we didn't choose. Whatever form they take, the invitation is the same: to listen more closely and meet ourselves with compassion.

My body has been my greatest teacher. It has urged me to listen to its wisdom and respond with care. Time and again, it has carried me back to a universal truth: I can always begin anew. That simple truth carries me forward, a quiet thread woven through my story and through the stories of all who are learning to trust the body's wisdom.

Healing, I've learned, is not perfection. It is presence. It is returning. It is the quiet courage to begin again in a way that acknowledges limits yet transcends them, expanding us in mysterious, unexpected ways. And perhaps that is the goal: to keep listening, softening, and evolving so that even in the unraveling of who we were before, we can find our way back home to ourselves.

Pause and Reflect

- Think about a time when your body gave you signals—through fatigue, tension, illness, or subtle unease—that you initially ignored. What was your body asking of you? Looking back, how might you have responded differently?

- How do you usually respond when life doesn't go according to plan—when you "fall"? What would it look like for you to rise again with compassion, rather than criticism?

- What does rest mean to you right now? Is there an area of your life where you might need to say "no," even if it feels difficult, in order to honor your well-being?

- Are there ways you have tried to change or control your body to feel "enough"? What would it mean to begin accepting your body for what it does for you, rather than how it looks?

- When have you leaned on others during a hard season? How did their support help you find strength you couldn't find on your own? Is there someone you might reach out to now, allowing yourself to be supported?

- In what area of your life do you feel called to "begin anew"? What small step could you take this week to honor that fresh start?

Part Four:
Embracing Our Shared Humanity

11

SHAME, SECRETS, AND SPEAKING OUR TRUTH

"When we are willing to be seen as we truly are, we offer the greatest gift of all: our authentic presence." — Tara Brach

This is not a chapter about food; it's about what happens when we name the truth—and what meets us on the other side. As I move into this part of my story, I am widening the lens. The truths I have struggled to face—shame, secrecy, the fear of not being enough—are not mine alone. They are human struggles, and they live quietly inside many of us.

For years, I let "healthy eating" and "good metabolism" hide what had already been named: fear and control wearing a wellness costume. What mattered now wasn't why I hid—it was what happened when I stopped hiding.

Stopping hiding didn't happen all at once; it began in moments like this.

I can still remember sitting in a support group meeting when a woman began praising my thinness. She went on and on about how she wished she could look like me, asking how I did it. I had just started opening up to my therapist about my struggles with food, so this woman's words struck a tender nerve. With each word of praise, a swell of anger and exhaustion rose in me, along with a desperate wish for her to stop.

I had never said the words out loud before, not to anyone. Still, something in me snapped. I broke the silence, my voice sharper than I expected: "I have an eating disorder."

Her response stunned me: "I wish I could get an eating disorder."

It was heartbreaking—not just because of her words, but because my moment of honesty left me feeling more invisible than ever. It seemed to confirm what I had feared all along: my thinness was what people valued most, not the person living inside my body. By saying "I have an eating disorder" aloud, a concealed truth emerged, and I felt suddenly exposed—raw and unmistakably seen, even as I disappeared in her response. For years, I smiled, deflected, and hid it. In that moment, the secret cracked wide open.

That meeting lingered with me. For so long, I feared that if people knew the truth, they would see me as broken, weak, or unlovable. Yet over time, I began to see that speaking it out loud hadn't destroyed me—it had set something in motion.

But movement doesn't mean arrival. The old habits of secrecy didn't vanish overnight. I continued to minimize, to deflect, to let others believe I was the one in control who always had it together. That was the role I knew how to play, and I convinced myself it was safer to keep playing it than to risk being seen. But each time I spoke honestly—to my therapist, to a trusted friend, or to my husband—a sliver of light pierced the darkness.

Even in the one moment when the truth slipped out unexpectedly, that light found its way in too.

The more I shared what was true and real, the less tightly those secrets held me.

Connection deepens when we let someone see the raw, unpolished parts of ourselves and we discover that love doesn't require perfection—it requires honesty.

I began to test that truth in the places that mattered most.

I shared the moment at the meeting with my therapist, still rattled by that woman's words, and by my own. I had spent years hiding behind the image of "healthy eating for MS" or pretending my thinness was "natural." By speaking the unspeakable out loud—*I have an eating disorder*—I exposed a part of myself I could never hide again. My therapist didn't flinch. Her steady presence helped me see that honesty doesn't push love away—it invites healing in. I began to see that shame loosens when it's spoken and met with empathy. Taking in that truth shifted my perspective, and the burden I had carried alone for so long began to lift. Secrets keep us locked away; truth opens the possibility for healing.

At first, my therapist was the only person I could be that open with. It was incredibly hard to let anyone else in. But her unwavering, non-judgmental presence gave me a glimpse of what it might feel like to tell the truth and still be loved. That glimpse mattered more than I knew.

Eventually, I opened up to my husband about what I had been hiding. I still remember the look on his face, the way he quickly said, "No you don't." His denial cut deep. For a moment, I felt dismissed, even foolish—a burden. I wished I hadn't spoken up at all.

Looking back now, I can see his reaction for what it was—fear, not rejection or cruelty. He was scared to admit his wife was struggling, scared of what it might mean. He simply wasn't ready to hear what I was ready to say.

His reaction, while painful, revealed a truth I think we all know deep down: whenever we speak honestly, we step into vulnerability, unsure of what might meet us on the other side. That is the risk of truth-telling: sometimes it opens doors, and sometimes it is met with walls. And when it's walls we meet, we are stung with the pain of rejection, or we recede into the loneliness of silence. For me, silence is the heavier burden. It disguises itself as safety, but ultimately it only deepens our isolation.

Each time I dared to speak my truth, I learned it wouldn't always be received the way I hoped. Sometimes there was silence, other times dismissal. Yet when love met my honesty, shame cracked open and something tender began to heal. The hardest part was finding the courage to keep offering my truth, even when it wasn't welcomed—remembering that someone else's refusal to hear me didn't mean I wasn't worth listening to.

For years, I kept most of my struggles with food hidden, even as I worked quietly with my therapist to untangle it all. Very few people knew the truth. By this time, my daughters were no longer little girls but young women finding their own voices. And then one day, it slipped out—not planned or polished, but blurted in a raw, unguarded moment—to my daughters. I braced for shame, for their disappointment, for the fear that honesty would push them away. Instead, they met me with love. Their words wrapped me with warmth and softened the shame I carried for years. What I feared would diminish me instead deepened our bond. In that moment, I knew I was enough—not perfect, but loved for who I was. That accidental message became a turning point; one I still carry. And maybe that is the hidden grace of honesty: the truths we most fear can sometimes become the very bridges that bring us closer.

For the longest time, I believed the safest thing was to keep my struggles hidden from my girls. —that if I appeared to have it all together, they'd never wrestle with food or body image like I did. I told myself that if I pretended it wasn't there, maybe it wouldn't ever touch their lives. That hope for my daughters came from love, even if it was misguided. But the truth has a way of finding its voice—bit by bit or all at once—whether we are ready or not.

The day it all spilled out, I had recorded a long voice message for a close friend I often confided in. I had just made the brave decision to work with a dietitian specializing in eating disorders. In my message, I shared how much of my life I spent struggling with food and how ready I was to get help. It was raw, vulnerable, and painfully honest. And then, with a single mistaken tap, I sent it to the wrong thread—the one with my two daughters.

The moment I realized what I had done, time seemed to stop. For a split second, my brain refused to believe it, as if denial could undo the mistake. Then the truth hit, and the floor gave way beneath me. My stomach dropped, my heart tightened, and a wave of panic surged through me. My hands shook so hard I could barely hold my phone. My body trembled with fear at what my daughters were about to discover.

Almost without thinking, I fumbled to record another message—this time for my daughters. My voice quivered as I tried to explain, "That message wasn't meant for you. It was for a friend" The words felt hollow—I knew there was no retrieving what had been said. The truth was out, and I was left exposed. How would they see me now? Would they resent me for having kept it hidden from them? After years of hiding behind the story that I was "just lucky" or had a "good metabolism," my secret was now laid bare before the people I had worked hardest to protect from it.

As I waited to hear back from the girls, the panic gave way to a gnawing fear—quieter but just as unsettling: the fear of being truly seen. Not the version of me I had worked so hard to present—the healthy, disciplined mom with the enviable metabolism—but the real me, with all of my struggles exposed. I worried this revelation would make me less in their eyes. Beneath it all was the persistent fear so many of us carry: if we are seen as we really are, we won't be enough.

When they called, I finally let the walls crumble. I answered their questions with honesty, and instead of judgment I was met with love and kindness. Each of my daughters, in their own way, told me how grateful they were that I was trusting them with the truth—and saddened to know I had carried it alone for so long. Their words wrapped me in warmth and softened the shame. What I feared would diminish me in their eyes instead deepened our bond. And in that moment, I knew I was enough. Not perfect, but perfectly imperfect. Loved not for the image I had worked so hard to uphold, but for the whole of who I was. Sometimes those unexpected moments of grace change everything.

I felt something shift. The secret I had guarded for decades no longer stood between us—it became a bridge. Instead of widening the distance, it drew us closer.

In that moment, I began to see that the real danger wasn't in being honest—it was in continuing to hide. Shame thrives in silence, but when we give voice to what we've hidden, its grip loosens. Even whispering the truth to one safe person can change how it lives in you.

That lesson didn't end with my daughters. Over time, I found the courage to let Todd in more fully. Years earlier, when I first confessed my struggles, his response was marked by shock and misunderstanding—he wasn't ready to hear it, and I wasn't going to press.

Over the years, we both grew. Through our own inner work and countless conversations, we learned how to listen without rushing to fix, how to speak with honesty, and how to hold space for one another. So, when I opened up about what I was working on in therapy and with my dietitian, I was met with love and compassion. Todd's support made all the difference, reminding me that healing never occurs in isolation; it only becomes possible when we allow ourselves to be held in love. Speaking my truth remained difficult, but each time I did, the burden grew lighter and healing found a way in.

Letting Todd in was both humbling and healing. Instead of carrying my struggle alone, I allowed him to see it up close—the fear, the painful daily work of eating more than felt possible, the slow steps toward change. Years earlier, he hadn't been able to hear me, and I bore the weight in silence. Now, he leaned in. He listened. He stood beside me. What once felt like a solitary battle became something shared, and the burden was no longer mine alone to carry.

Sharing honestly was a risk I was finally willing to take. Pretending had only kept me stuck. If you've ever risked sharing after having been shut down, you know how much courage it takes to open that door a second time. But when love meets you on the other side, it makes every ounce of risk worth it.

The same was true with my daughters. Once my secret was out, there was no going back to pretending. And as frightening as that was at first, it made change possible. Their compassion helped me see myself through gentler more loving eyes, reminding me I didn't need to be perfect to be enough.

My story isn't mine alone—it belongs to all of us. We all carry secrets. The details may differ, but the weight of hiding is universal. It wears on us invisibly, creating a loneliness that deepens the longer we hold it. But when we dare to speak what we have hidden, we remember we are not the only ones. In remembering, we touch the truth of our shared humanity.

In those moments—whether in quiet conversations with Todd or in hearing our daughters' words of encouragement—I am reminded that recovery cannot happen in isolation.

While shame urges us to hide, connection encourages us to heal.

When we speak what we've hidden, we don't just free ourselves—we open the door for others.

Being seen didn't break me. It brought me home.

Pause and Reflect

- Is there something in your life you have kept hidden out of shame or fear of judgment? What has holding it in cost you—emotionally, physically, or in your relationships?

- Who do you feel safe enough with to share your truth? What would it feel like to reveal just one small piece of what you have been holding?

- Think of a time when you spoke your truth, even in a small way. What shifted inside of you, or between you and others, when you brought it into the light?

- If shame grows in the dark, what is one step you could take this week to allow a little more light in?

- Despite the risk of rejection, how might you come to see vulnerability as a bridge to connection instead of weakness? What gentle step might you take this week to invite more connection into your life?

12

MINDFULNESS AS A LIFELONG PRACTICE

"The present moment is filled with joy and happiness. If you are attentive, you will see it." —Thich Nhat Hanh

Mindfulness has never been a quick fix. It has not erased my illness, taken away my fears, or guaranteed a smooth path ahead. What it has given me is a steady ground to return to: a way of coming back to myself—and choosing how I want to meet whatever life brings. Some days that return to self looks like pausing to notice my breath before a doctor's appointment. Other days it consists of placing my hand on my heart after a hard conversation. And just as often, it means being awake to joy, resting in the quiet assurance that I am here, and knowing this moment is enough.

It is easy to imagine mindfulness as something reserved for meditation cushions and quiet rooms. But the truth is, any moment can become a mindfulness practice when we bring our full attention to it. Ordinary moments—ones we might otherwise overlook—can become powerful doorways into practice. Even something as small and ordinary as a raisin can open the doorway to presence.

In my classes, I sometimes guide people through the raisin exercise. It's simple—we each hold a single raisin in our hand. At first, there is a ripple of laughter; it seems silly that so much attention could be given to something so small. But as we slow our breathing down, something shifts. We pause to notice the wrinkles, the stickiness against our fingers, the hint of a sweet aroma. Finally, we taste—slowly, with curiosity. What always strikes me is how quickly the room grows quiet. The raisin, ordinary and overlooked, becomes a reminder of what it means to *be here now*—and how even the smallest moments in our daily lives can hold unexpected depth when met with our full attention. This kind of attention can be given to folding laundry, savoring the flavors of a meal, or walking outside and feeling the rhythm of each step. When we bring all of our senses to an activity, the most ordinary moments reveal a richness often missed.

The raisin, the laundry, the walk outside—teach us that mindfulness doesn't require waiting for the "right" conditions. It's less about creating extra time in the day and more about inhabiting the time we already have. The present moment is all we truly have—the place where life itself unfolds.

The laundry and the walk are mindfulness in motion; the cushion is mindfulness in stillness. Meditation is the more formal way of practicing mindfulness. When we sit, the practice is simply to notice the activity of the mind. Each time we realize our attention has wandered, we gently—without judgment—bring it back to the breath, the body, and the present moment.

You might think of meditation as exercise for the brain, like a mental bicep curl: every return to the breath strengthens our capacity to be here now. Over time, that repetition builds something invaluable—creating a sort of pause. In that space, we find the freedom to respond with awareness rather than react from old beliefs or habits that no longer serve us. Neuroscience shows that each return to the breath and body forms new pathways in the brain, allowing us to relate to stress from a more grounded, steady place.

Formal mindfulness practice through meditation and informal practice—bringing all of our senses to everyday activities—are not separate paths but vital partners in the same journey. Together, they weave mindfulness into every part of life—reminding us that presence isn't something to wait for; it is available in every ordinary moment.

Over time, I saw that mindfulness wasn't just for tuning into certain moments—it was something that could carry me through life. The time I spent on the cushion strengthened me for daily life, and the challenges of daily life kept sending me back to the cushion. Slowly, the line between the two began to blur. What once felt like separate practices became one steady rhythm—a way of living that wove presence through both the ordinary and the extraordinary, the joyful and the painful.

Mindfulness isn't something to check off or master; it is a way of living—a practice I return to again and again. Some days it feels natural, almost effortless—like slipping into a comfortable pair of old shoes. Other days it feels wobbly, as if I'm breaking in a pair of high heels. But that's the point: mindfulness isn't about doing it perfectly. It is about returning with compassion and without expectation or attachment to how things should or should not be.

For me, teaching mindfulness is inseparable from practicing it. What I share with others is exactly what I need to keep practicing myself. Sharing keeps it real for me, reminding me that I receive as much as I give. Teaching these practices heals me too—helping me return, remember, and grow. The connection it creates is its own gift, showing me that no one walks this path alone.

Through every season of my life—relapses and remissions, celebrations and losses—this practice has been both anchor and compass. As anchor, it steadies me when fear or uncertainty threatens to pull me off course. As compass, it guides me back to what matters most: presence, connection, compassion.

We all have places that test our steadiness. For me, it is often the doctor's office—the waiting rooms, the tests, the conversations that can alter the course of the day. For someone else, it might be a looming deadline, a long commute, or waiting for difficult news. These are the spaces where stress and uncertainty can tighten the body and send the mind spinning. And in harder seasons—especially during relapses when MS makes the familiar feel unpredictable—the weight can be overwhelming. That's when mindfulness becomes my anchor. A breath. The feel of my feet on the floor. A hand resting over my heart. Sometimes it's a whisper of gratitude—the kindness of a nurse, the warmth of a blanket, the stabilizing force of the breath. These small gestures don't undo the circumstances, but they transform the way I meet them. They remind me that I am here, I am held, and I am not alone.

When we learn to meet our own hearts with presence, that same presence flows outward into how we meet others—especially in moments of conflict. We have all experienced hard conversations, and we often react from fear, insecurity, or the urge to control the outcome. Mindfulness helps us slow down—to pause. In that pause, we can notice what's rising inside—fear, sadness, anger—and get curious about the tender place beneath the emotion before responding. We can take a breath, imagine the perspective of the other person, and listen more fully. The pause doesn't erase the difficulty, but it softens its sharpness. It makes room for empathy—for ourselves and for the other person. Rooted in compassion, we can respond from a more grounded, peaceful place—one that opens the door to deeper connection.

Daily life brings its own kind of stress—traffic, deadlines, packed schedules. In those ordinary moments, mindfulness offers simple anchors like taking a slow breath at a red light, noticing the warmth of the sun, or taking a slow sip of tea before opening the next email. It can be as subtle as feeling the ground beneath your feet when the day feels chaotic. It doesn't take an hour of practice to shift how you feel in your body—sometimes one mindful moment is enough. These pauses help us remember that we don't have to wait for life to be calm in order to feel steady. Steadiness is available in the simple act of coming back to the present moment.

When choices or challenges arise, mindfulness, like a compass, points me in the right direction. When I'm facing a difficult decision, it quiets the noise of overthinking and helps me return to the wisdom of my body and breath. When I'm with someone I love, it directs me toward presence—toward holding space instead of rushing to fix and toward compassion instead of control. It doesn't erase difficult emotions, but it grounds me in the midst of them and reassures me I don't have to have everything figured out. Again and again, it points me to what matters most: love, connection, and the simple grace of knowing this moment is enough.

Over the years, mindfulness has taught me that life is not something to master or control, but something to be met by resting in the truth of this moment. And when I can rest there, it softens the need to fix and allows the space to simply be.

To practice mindfulness is to practice belonging—to ourselves, to one another, and to the present moment where all of life unfolds. Of course, I don't always remember. I forget, I fall back into old habits, I react in ways I wish I hadn't. But even these experiences are part of the practice. They are part of the process of beginning again with compassion and the trust that I am enough.

Mindfulness has brought about the realization that I don't always have to be accomplishing or doing. For so much of my life, I measured my worth by how productive I was, how much I could push through, and how well I could hold everything together. But mindfulness invited me into a different way of living—one rooted not in striving, but in simply being. It has taught me how to connect with my breath, inhabit my body with care, and meet each unfolding moment with openness and grace. In the end, mindfulness asks not for perfection, but for presence. It invites us to soften into acceptance of what is here and to remember that even in the midst of struggle, joy and happiness are still quietly present—waiting to be seen.

Pause and Reflect

- Think of an ordinary task you do every day—washing dishes, brushing your teeth, making the bed. How might you turn it into a moment of mindfulness by bringing all five senses to the experience?

- Recall a recent time when you felt stressed, hurried, or overwhelmed. How might pausing—even for one breath—have changed the way you moved through that moment?

- Where in your life do you notice the pull toward *doing*—toward proving, producing, or perfecting? How might you give yourself permission, even briefly, to rest in simply *being*?

- What anchors help you steady yourself when life feels uncertain? What compass points you to what matters most?

- Joy is often quieter than we expect. Where in your days do you catch glimpses of joy, waiting to be noticed?

13

TRUSTING LIFE'S UNFOLDING

"The way to get through your own fear is to trust that life has a plan for you, even if you can't see it yet." — *Martha Beck*

Trust, at its heart, is a form of surrender—not giving up, but loosening our grip on the life we thought we were meant to live so we can step into the one that is unfolding. For me, that loosening often began on a blank page. Since childhood, journaling has been my refuge—the place I could whisper truths too scary to say aloud. I kept a small brass-key diary tucked in my nightstand, filling its pages with the secret thoughts of a girl trying to make sense of her world and daring to dream of who she might one day be. But even then, fear shadowed me. I kept my words locked and hidden, as though the truth inside them needed protecting. And when each diary was full, I tore out pages and buried them deep in the trash, never to be read.

What I feared most was the possibility of being seen. And beneath that fear was shame in disguise: the quiet belief so many of us carry—that if our truth was known, we might be perceived as too much of one thing and not enough of another.

As I grew older, the ritual continued: fill the journals, then rip out the pages before anyone could read them. The fear was irrational, but powerful—the belief that if someone found those words after I was gone, they would be disappointed in me. More than that, I was afraid of being misunderstood. Sure, I wanted someone to know me, but only the version I could control. I could be honest and safe within the pages of my journal where no one would ever read a word. Many of us know that fear: the worry that our truest thoughts, if exposed, might somehow make us less in the eyes of those we love. Still, writing kept pulling me back to the part of me that wanted to be known.

In middle school, I sat in English class dreaming of the day I would write a book. I didn't know what kind of book—perhaps a crime mystery—but I knew this: I felt most like myself when I was writing. I sensed that writing might be a hidden gift that could one day help me, and others, make sense of the world.

My writing lived mostly on the pages of private journals well into adulthood. But not long after my diagnosis, a strange clarity surfaced amid the fear and uncertainty: one day, I will write my story. The thought didn't arrive as a plan, but as a conviction, and the image of a book cover began to form in my mind.

A title popped into my head: *MySelf*, with the letters MS in bold type, standing both for multiple sclerosis and for the deeper work of learning to see myself more clearly. The phrase *I lost my sight so that I could see* landed in my heart. Having lost vision in one eye during a relapse, I meant it literally. But more so, I was starting to see inward in a way I never had before: to notice what needed healing, what mattered, and how much of my life had been shaped by trying to be what others wanted me to be.

Ironically, losing sight became the doorway to learning how to truly see myself. Writing about my journey wasn't meant to create a polished story, but to share a truth. If it rippled outward, touching even one other person, I knew I would find the meaning I longed for in my journey.

One day, after sharing my history of locked journals and the persistent fear of people reading my story, my therapist asked me, gently but directly, "What might happen if someone read your journal after you died?" My reflexive response was a rush of unreasonable fears. She asked, simply, "And then what?" Her question hung in the air, unsettling and liberating all at once. For the first time, I imagined my story surviving me—not as something shameful, but as something human. That one question, and the image it conjured, shifted everything. I suddenly realized I no longer wanted to spend my life shredding my story. So, I showed up, imperfectly, to face the blank pages that eventually became this book and began to loosen the old habit of hiding. I now knew my voice could hold both shame *and* dignity, and that being seen made me no less lovable.

I still grieve those torn or shredded pages—I would give anything to sit with that little girl's journals and see how far she's come. Still, there is a consolation: this book, in a way, has gathered those tattered fragments. Where I once threw my life away in bits, I am now choosing to keep it whole. A new journal sits on my bedside table. I do not hide it. There is no lock now, no key to guard or lose. The impulse to tear up pages has diminished; in its place is trust that my words can stand as they are.

I trust that if my daughters stumble upon my journals one day, they won't see someone to judge or fix, but a mother who was real, human, and still growing. Perhaps in those pages they will find a hidden treasure—a record of a woman learning, stumbling, and rising again. And maybe, as they turn those pages, they will see what I have come to see: that even in our messiness, we are whole.

Trust doesn't grow only in quiet self-reflections or on the page. It is tested most when life veers off script—when the ground shifts beneath our feet and we are asked to walk forward anyway. Again and again, MS has been a teacher showing me that trust is less about certainty and more about how we meet the unknown.

One day, I was moving through the ordinary rhythm of errands and appointments; the next, my body changed without warning. It happened suddenly, as relapses often do. My legs grew heavy, my vision blurred, and even the simple act of crossing the room was a challenge. It felt like elastic bands were cinched tightly around my lower body, making every step stiff and constrained. Like wading through quicksand, each movement dragged me deeper. Each step carried the weight of not knowing—how long will it last, how much will it take from me, how many more times do I have to start again? Dizziness pressed in and balance slipped away.

I had lived through this before—the shock, the sinking dread, the desperate thought: *Oh no, not again.* Every plan for the week dissolved in an instant; the calendar proved no longer relevant. Control slipped through my fingers, leaving only the raw truth of the present. I didn't know how serious it would be or what it might cost me physically and emotionally. And so, the cycle began again: the call to the neurologist, the likely order for an MRI, the waiting, the difficult decisions.

I had learned, through trial and error, that trust mattered most—trust that I could just let things unfold. And that minimizing stress was the single most helpful gift I could offer my body while letting the relapse run its course. In moments like those, my instinct was always to fight—to tighten, to resist, to demand answers. Sometimes that resistance looked like frantic organizing: rearranging a closet, imposing order wherever I could. When life inside my body felt unpredictable, creating order outside provided a fleeting sense of control. I think we all desperately grasp for what can be managed when so much cannot.

But no amount of neatly stacked containers could change what was happening in my body. What it needed wasn't control, but care. Not a step stool to reach the top shelf, but restorative, unapologetic rest. For years, I equated the stillness of rest with weakness, but slowly I realized that rest can be a form of strength—a quiet act of trusting.

When I loosened my grip on control and surrendered to trust, rest became possible. Certainly, trust doesn't mean liking what is happening or pretending it is easy. It means softening into the present reality rather than clinging to the one I wish I was in. Trust lays out a welcome mat for whatever arises—fear, grief, frustration—and affirms that even in uncertain moments, we are held.

Sometimes that looked as ordinary as placing a hand over my heart and whispering, *this is hard, and I am OK*. Other times it meant closing my eyes, feeling the rhythm of my breath, and letting the tears come without shame. Trust also meant reaching out to the people in my circle who reminded me I was not carrying this alone. Over and over, I discovered that loosening my grasp allowed a steadiness I could not find through control.

During that relapse, I did what I had learned to do. I followed my neurologist's directives, leaned on my mindfulness practices, and reached out for support. Canceling a trip to see a dear friend was heartbreaking, but her warmth gave me the permission I still struggled to give myself: to step back and rest. And as with every relapse, I was reminded of the quiet gifts of letting go: the benefit of giving myself healing time, the strength of community, and the stabilizing presence of faith. Trust, I realized once more, isn't about escaping difficulty but meeting it head on. During life's hardest seasons, what carries us is not control, but connection, faith, and the willingness to remain open to possibilities, solutions—a new reality.

Trust is not blind optimism or denying the pain of what is happening. It is choosing to stay present in the midst of it. When certainty disappears, we can lean into love, connection, and the steady rhythm of breath to carry us through. Trusting life's unfolding is rarely simple. It asks us to loosen our grip when everything in us wants to hold tighter. To keep walking when the path ahead is unclear. To keep listening when silence is unbearable. Most of all, it asks us to soften our hearts and meet life as it is when it looks nothing like what we had planned.

For me, trust is the common thread that has shown up in many places—in relapses that forced me to slow down, in the courage it took to write this book, in the decision to stop tearing up my journals. Through it all, I've come to see that trust is not a single decision—it is a practice. Life has repeatedly asked me to release the illusion of control and step into the unknown with open arms. Trust has never come without fear, but when I soften into it, something larger than fear holds me. Trust has become the choice to no longer lock myself away. The miracle is that when we dare to bring our whole selves, life meets us there—sometimes with fear still in the room, but also with unexpected beauty and grace.

Trust continues to ask for my participation—to keep saying yes to life even when it doesn't go as planned. In my experience, the unexpected way life unfolds is not the obstacle, but the invitation: a quiet call to meet each new moment with curiosity and trust instead of fear.

"Trust is not the absence of fear, but the willingness to keep stepping forward even when the path is unclear." —from my journal

Pause and Reflect

- Recall a time when life diverged from the path you had planned. What helped you release control and discover steadiness in the midst of uncertainty?

- Despite not knowing what comes next, where in your life right now are you being invited to trust?

- Think of a moment when something unexpected carried a hidden gift. How might that memory remind you that grace can live in uncertainty?

- Like torn-out journal pages, what parts of yourself have you been tempted to keep hidden? What might become possible if those parts were brought into the light with compassion?

- Imagine meeting the unknown as a companion instead of an enemy. How might that shift the way you move through today?

14

THE GIFTS WE CARRY FORWARD

"In the end, just three things matter: How well we have lived. How well we have loved. How well we have learned to let go." — Jack Kornfield

When I look back over these pages, what strikes me most is not the stories themselves but the thread that runs through them—how each season, each stumble, each moment of grace has left behind something valuable. We don't often recognize those gifts while we're in the middle of the unraveling. But with time, we may come to see how our most fragile places have become part of the foundation we stand on now.

The lessons I have learned on my journey through MS arrived in many forms. Illness taught me to release control. Loss asked me to soften in ways I didn't know I could. Recovery taught me that wholeness is not found in perfection, but in the steady practice of compassion, connection, and self-trust. Time and again, the practice of mindfulness revealed that healing is not a single destination but a way of meeting myself—with honesty, patience, and care.

These experiences didn't cancel my fears or erase my struggles. They gave me something more enduring: the reminder that even in the hardest seasons, life shapes us. Slowly, almost tenderly, the very places we once wanted to keep hidden have become teachers, holding unexpected lessons and gifts. And if we pay attention, we may find that our most fragile places quietly offer something worth carrying.

It is those gifts I want to share with you now. Not as rules to follow, but as companions that mindfulness has given me along the way. They are the touchstones I return to when life feels uncertain, and I offer them here hoping you recognize their presence in your own journey. Over time, I've come to see that these companions are not found in any single practice, but in the quiet ways mindfulness weaves itself through daily life—in the pause before reacting, the breath that steadies the mind, the choice to meet oneself with care. Looking back, what mindfulness has offered me is not a single answer, but a handful of treasures I return to again and again. These gifts have carried me through illness, uncertainty, and change—and they continue to guide me in the ordinary rhythm of daily life.

The Gift of Presence

Presence is the simplest gift yet the hardest to hold. It asks nothing of us but to arrive—here, now, with what is. This gift teaches us that life is not lived in a past we cannot change or a future we cannot control, but in the breath within us. It is found in the steady beat of our heart, the brush of fabric against skin, the rhythm of footsteps meeting the earth. Presence has taught me that every moment, no matter how ordinary, can be sacred when met with attention. It's not about escaping life, but learning to truly inhabit it—to feel the texture of each moment as it unfolds.

Reader invitation: Pause now. Take one slow breath. Feel the weight of your body where it rests, the air moving in and out. Notice the sounds around you, the light and color in the room, even the faintest scents. Presence isn't something you have to earn—it is always waiting for you.

And from presence, a new sensitivity begins to take root—the gift of being able to turn our gentle attention inward.

The Gift of Self-Compassion

For years, I offered compassion easily to others but struggled to extend the same kindness to myself. The gift of self-compassion is learning that I too am worthy of the tenderness I give so freely. It has shown me that care begins within—that when I soften toward myself, I find a steadiness no amount of striving can bring. Each time I meet myself with gentleness, I loosen the old belief that worth must be earned. This gift has shown me that I can be both a work in progress and enough, exactly as I am.

Reader invitation: Place a hand gently over your heart. Take a slow breath and whisper to yourself, "*I am worthy of my own kindness.*" Let the words settle in, as if you were offering comfort to a dear friend. Notice how it feels to turn compassion inward, letting it root quietly within.

Compassion softens our edges, and in that softening, we begin to loosen our grip—making space for trust to enter.

The Gift of Trust

Trust asks us to loosen our grip on certainty and let life unfold in its own time. It does not mean the fear vanishes or we stop caring—it means we keep showing up, even when the way forward is unclear. For me, trust has meant learning to rest when my body grows weary, to let words keep flowing even when doubt is loud, to reach outward for support instead of folding inward. Trust has become the still hand I place over my heart when uncertainty rises—the reminder that I don't have to see the whole picture to take the next step. This gift has shown me that steadiness isn't born of control, but of meeting the unknown with a heart open enough to receive it.

Reader invitation: Rest your palms open on your lap. Take a breath and feel the gentle release that comes with not holding so tightly. Imagine the next step in your life unfolding, even if you cannot see the whole path. Trust that you do not need all the answers to keep moving forward.

Trusting life also invites us to focus inward—to listen for the quiet wisdom already there.

The Gift of Wisdom Within

The Gift of Wisdom Within reveals that guidance runs deeper than conscious thought. My body, my breath, my heart—all carry signals if I am willing to pay attention. Sometimes it comes as a heaviness asking me to slow down, other times as a lightness nudging me forward. This gift teaches that true wisdom doesn't come from forcing or fixing, but from honoring the quiet knowing already alive inside us.

Reader invitation: Close your eyes and ask your body, "*What do you need right now?*" Wait in stillness, without rushing to answer. Notice what sensation, image, or whisper arises. Trust that it has something to tell you.

When we pause to listen, gratitude rises naturally—revealing the inner beauty already here.

The Gift of Gratitude

Gratitude has been the thread of gold woven through my hardest days. It doesn't erase pain, but it reminds me that beauty and struggle often live side by side—that in the midst of difficulty, there is always something worth noticing: the quiet hum of life continuing, the touch of a hand, the gentle patter of rain on the roof. Gratitude turns our gaze from what is missing to what is here, reminding us that most moments in life are worth savoring. Gratitude doesn't deny what is hard—it teaches us to hold both the ache and the light, to let them shape us into something more fully whole.

Reader invitation: Bring to mind one small thing—right now—that you are grateful for. Let it fill your awareness for a few breaths. Notice how your body softens as you rest in appreciation. Imagine gratitude as a golden thread weaving light through your day.

Gratitude, in its subtle way, draws us home—to belonging, to the awareness that we are held within something larger than ourselves. It reminds us that even when life feels uncertain, we were never meant to carry it all alone.

The Gift of Connection

Connection is another thread that weaves through us all—linking us back to ourselves and to one another. It affirms that healing is never a solitary journey—we are shaped in the presence of others. This gift has shown me that I don't need to carry everything by myself. Whether through shared laughter, honest tears, or simply sitting side by side, connection reminds us that we don't have to walk alone—and in that knowing, the path feels steadier, safer—possible.

Reader invitation: Think of someone who has walked beside you in a meaningful way. Picture their face, their presence, and the way you felt less alone because they were there. Hold them in your heart with gratitude. If it feels right, reach out with a note, a call, or even a silent blessing: *"Thank you for walking this path with me."* Notice how connection, when magnified by gratitude, makes the journey lighter and more enjoyable. Focusing on the gifts of connection and gratitude allows us to see them as parts of a larger whole—threads woven together to create a way of living that continues to carry us forward.

Presence, Self-Compassion, Trust, Wisdom Within, Gratitude, and Connection are six incredible gifts that mindfulness gave me over the years. They are there for all of us—to meet us in our ordinary days, steady us in uncertainty, and help us notice grace moving through our lives. I have not always received these gifts easily. Some came slowly, through steady practice and trial and error. Others revealed themselves in the darker seasons—when illness weighed heavy, grief ran deep, and uncertainty clouded the way forward. Yet even there, they took root and reshaped my life. Each one arrived as both a teacher and a mirror, revealing what I most needed to remember: that healing is less about striving and more about returning—again and again—to my perfectly imperfect self. They taught me that healing is not about fixing what is broken but about learning to be whole in the midst of it all.

As you leave these pages, may you carry these gifts in your own way—once again, not as hard, fast rules but as companion guides to walk beside you. Let presence ground you in the here and now. Let self-compassion soften the harsh edges of your inner critic. Lean on trust when control slips away. Listen to the wisdom alive within you. Let gratitude gently return your awareness to the quiet beauty in each moment. And allow connection to guide you back to the essential truth: you were never meant to walk alone.

The path may not always be clear, but when we dare to bring our whole selves—tender, imperfect, and luminous—life meets us with more grace than we could have imagined. So may you keep moving gently through your days, one breath, one step, one word at a time. May you trust the unfolding of your own journey. And may you always carry this truth close to your heart: you are enough, exactly as you are.

Pause and Reflect

Take a few moments to consider the six gifts—Presence, Self-Compassion, Trust, Wisdom Within, Gratitude, and Connection.

- Notice which gift feels closest to your heart right now.

- Ask yourself: *Which one do I need most in this season of my life?*

- Imagine carrying that gift with you into tomorrow, letting it walk beside you as a quiet companion. How might that change your perspective about the future?

- Remember that all six exist within you, waiting to be called upon whenever the path feels uncertain.

15

LIVING MINDFULLY EVERY DAY

"The little things? The little moments? They aren't little." — Jon Kabat-Zinn

The first time I stood before a room of students to teach a mindfulness introductory series, my heart pounded, my palms went damp, and my voice trembled in ways I could not hide. I wasn't a teacher, not really —at least that's what I told myself. The owner of the mindfulness center had encouraged me to teach after hearing how mindfulness had transformed my life, trusting that my lived experience would speak more deeply than any formal training ever could.

Still, as I stood before that group, doubt crept in. Who was I to guide others when I was still learning myself?

As I began to speak, my mind went blank. Panic rose—that familiar tightening in my chest, the quickening of the breath. And then, somewhere inside the swirl, I remembered what I was there to share: Pause. Breathe. Be present.

I took one slow, deliberate breath followed by another. I softened my shoulders, felt my feet on the floor, and allowed myself to speak—not from training or theory, but from lived experience. In that moment, something opened. The words came easily, not because I had mastered mindfulness, but because I was *practicing* it—right there, in real time.

That day reminded me that mindfulness doesn't ask us to be perfect. It simply invites us to begin again, right where we are—shaky voice and all. I learned that mindfulness isn't about saying the right thing or doing it correctly. It's about meeting each moment as it unfolds—with honesty, curiosity, and care. Each breath, each moment of awareness, is enough.

That first teaching experience reminded me that mindfulness doesn't only happen in stillness or silence—it happens in the middle of everyday life. Each moment offers an invitation to return to presence: while making coffee, driving to work, speaking to a friend, or feeling the first stirrings of stress. These are the moments where the practice comes alive—not as something separate from living, but as the way we live.

While we can practice anywhere, setting aside time for intentional stillness each day deepens the way we move through life. Time on the cushion—those moments of quiet, dedicated practice—strengthens the awareness we carry into daily life as we move, speak, and respond. The goal is not to escape the world, but to meet it with steadiness and care. The two forms work together—one grounding us in presence, the other allowing that presence to ripple through all we do.

My own practice begins before I even get out of bed. Each morning, I take a few slow, mindful stretches—gentle movements that help ease stiffness and welcome the day. Instead of rushing ahead, I stay with the sensations: muscles waking, breath steadying, a quiet gratitude for the parts of me that show up each day. Before standing, I set an intention—a simple phrase that reflects how I want to move through the day.

This practice has become a small daily ritual of appreciation and grounding—one that reminds me to start each day with awareness, presence, and a sense of choice. From there, mindfulness continues into the simplest moments, where something as ordinary as getting dressed becomes an invitation to come home to your senses.

Each morning begins like a quiet rehearsal for how I want to move through the day—awake, steady, and attuned to what's here. As I move from the bed to the sink, I carry that same awareness with me. Even the smallest moments—like brushing my teeth—can become gateways to presence. As I brush, I notice the feel of the toothbrush in my hand, the cool mint on my tongue, the texture of the paste, the sound of water running in the sink. Paying attention in this way transforms a task I've done thousands of times into a quiet, grounding moment of peace.

I try to bring that same awareness to other parts of daily life—making dinner or taking a walk. What once felt like chores now feel like invitations to be fully present. Preparing a meal becomes a sensory meditation—the vivid colors of the vegetables, the crisp sound of the knife, the aroma rising from the pan. On a walk, I feel my feet meet the earth and the breeze caress my skin. Attention turns tasks into moments of presence.

That same awareness naturally extends into the rhythm of work—answering emails, preparing for meetings, pausing before I speak. I notice the feel of my fingers on the keyboard, the cadence of voices in conversation, the subtle way my body softens after one mindful breath. The practice itself doesn't change; only the circumstances we bring it to. Each pause, each conscious breath, becomes a quiet reminder that presence is always available, wherever we are.

Living mindfully isn't about adding something extra to your day—its' about showing up for what's already here, with attention and care. What matters isn't what you practice, but how you practice: with compassion, without judgment or expectation, and with moments and rituals that flow naturally and nourish you.

Perhaps, for you, it is a morning cup of tea, time in the garden, or a few deep breaths before opening your laptop. There is no single right way. The most meaningful practice is the one you return to with curiosity and care, again and again.

As we learn to bring mindfulness into daily life, something subtle begins to change. The pauses come more easily and the awareness lingers a little longer. We start to notice not only what is happening *around* us, but also what is unfolding *within* us—the thoughts, emotions, and reactions shaping how we move through the world. This is where the outer and inner meet— mindfulness moves from what we are *doing* to how we are *being*. The same curiosity and kindness we bring to brushing our teeth or walking the dog can begin to meet our thoughts, our feelings, and our tender inner landscape.

As awareness expands inward, it also begins to reach outward. The way we meet ourselves becomes the way we meet others. Over time, I noticed that mindfulness wasn't only changing how I moved through my day—it was changing how I showed up with others. The same awareness that steadied me through the rhythm of my days began to soften my communication, deepening the way I listened and connected.

In the space between two people, mindfulness becomes a living practice. Presence transforms communication more than almost anything else. When I pause before speaking or listen without planning my next words, there is more space for understanding. I notice the tone of my voice, the expression on the other person's face, the subtle currents of emotion underneath. Listening this way is tender work; it asks for vulnerability, the willingness to be changed by what we hear, and the courage to respond with kindness. Mindfulness invites us to listen not just with our ears, but with our hearts—to meet others with the same gentle curiosity we are learning to extend to ourselves.

Of course, knowing about the pause and living it are two very different things. Some of my greatest lessons in mindfulness have come from the moments I've stumbled—especially in how I listen and speak with those I love most. My husband would tell me, often with frustration, that I tended to interrupt him during moments of conflict. Understandably, my interrupting made him feel unimportant, and his irritation then triggered my old pattern of retreating to keep the peace. It became a loop: his frustration sparked my fear; my fear fed my urgency to speak.

Mindfulness helped me see the pattern and feel it in my body—the familiar rush of urgency in my body, the pull to react, the impulse to jump in. When I could pause, open, and truly listen, something eased inside. It wasn't instant or perfect, but awareness gave me options, and vulnerability invited me to stay present. When I stayed present long enough to really hear, I found more compassion, and compassion made kinder responses possible.

The first step wasn't changing my behavior—it was noticing what was happening inside me. As I learned to pause and observe those sensations without judgment, I began to find the space to choose another way. I would take a breath, relax my body, and listen—really listen.

It isn't always easy. Old habits have deep roots, and in moments of stress, they tend to resurface. But now, awareness gives me choices. I can choose to stay present instead of reacting. I can trust that if what I want to say is truly important, it will still be there when it's my turn. This simple shift—from reacting to choosing—has changed how I communicate and how I show up in my relationships. When I can be fully present in this way, my husband feels heard—and that same presence allows me to show up more calmly and connected in all of my relationships, more grounded in my own body.

Mindful listening can be surprisingly hard. Notice what gets in the way of listening with an open heart: fixing, defending, planning the next line. Expect those impulses; then let them go and choose to stay present.

This is the quiet magic of mindfulness in relationship: when we bring our full attention and open hearts to another, we create the space where being seen and understood becomes its own kind of healing.

The space we create for others becomes the space we learn to hold for ourselves.

It is in the ordinary moments that the heart of mindfulness is revealed: awareness and compassion. Mindfulness helps us see the patterns that shape our reactions—the ways we protect, defend, or rush to control. Awareness itself can feel uncomfortable at first; it asks us to face what we might rather avoid. But when we meet that awareness with kindness instead of criticism, something softens.

We stop fighting ourselves. We begin to see that awareness isn't the end of the practice—it is the beginning of a kinder relationship with ourselves.

Staying present with what we find takes practice. It is the quiet work of courage—the willingness to look inward with an open heart. Each time we pause long enough to notice and breathe, we strengthen that inner muscle of compassion, allowing us to be gentler with ourselves and, in turn, with others.

As we begin to look inward with mindfulness, we start to see how automatic many of our reactions are. The pause gives us room to witness what is really happening beneath the surface—the thought patterns, emotional habits, and old stories that quietly shape us. From here, we learn to meet what we find with compassion, remembering that the goal isn't to fix or change ourselves, but to see with kindness. When we pause long enough to respond instead of react, mindfulness begins to transform us from the inside out.

Allow me to restate this most important point: There is a moment—the briefest pause—between what happens and how we respond. That is where mindfulness lives. That pause—small as it is—can change everything. It is the space where awareness becomes choice. As Viktor Frankl so beautifully expressed, "Between the stimulus and the response there is a space. In that space lies our power to choose our response. In our response lies our growth and our freedom."

When I share this with students, I often draw it as a picture: the word *stimulus* on one side of the board, *response* on the other, with a small space between them. I call that space *the magic pause*—the place where awareness turns into freedom. It's rarely dramatic.

Sometimes it's just one breath, a softening of the shoulders, a heartbeat's worth of awareness before words leave the mouth.

One of my students, an attorney, once shared how he began using a simple reminder to pause during particularly stressful days at work. He wasn't proud of how reactive he tended to be with his assistant—his tone sharp, his patience thin—and it was straining their relationship. After one class, he decided to draw a small stop sign on the back of his hand, a cue to stop and take a breath before responding.

When he returned the following week, he said the difference was remarkable. Not only did he feel calmer and more in control, but his assistant had noticed too. That tiny reminder to pause had eased the tension in their interactions and lightened the energy of their days.

It's striking how something so small—a breath, a symbol, a single moment of awareness—can transform everything. The pause doesn't stop life—it reminds us to meet it with presence. In everyday life, that space can feel impossibly small. My husband, for example, can get frustrated in traffic when someone cuts him off. The reaction is instant—hands tightening on the wheel, breath shortening, irritation rising. We all have our versions of that: moments when we move straight from stimulus to reaction without even realizing it.

But mindfulness invites us to notice what's happening as it is happening. Perhaps instead of shouting or weaving through traffic, he could take a breath, loosen his grip, and remember that the other driver might be having a hard day—that their behavior likely has nothing to do with him. The situation doesn't change, but the space inside does. That pause creates room for choice—for a calmer, kinder response. Practiced often enough, this can transform not just our mood, but the quality of our days and relationships.

That is what awareness offers us: a moment of freedom from habitual reactions. We begin to see our patterns—the ways we grasp for control, rush to please, strive for perfection, or push away discomfort. I sometimes joke that I'm a recovering perfectionist and people-pleaser. Those habits once made me feel safe, as if vigilance could keep life safe and predictable. But mindfulness showed me how exhausting that was—and how peace can grow in the gentle space of letting go.

Learning to let go didn't happen in a single moment of insight—it was a gradual unwinding, one small situation at a time. I still see it in the smallest moments—when plans change unexpectedly, when my body asks for rest sooner than I'd hoped, when technology falters just as I'm finding my rhythm. Each time, awareness offers a choice: to tense and resist, or to breathe and allow. The more I practice pausing in those moments, the more I realize that peace doesn't come from controlling what happens—it comes from softening into what is.

That is the quiet power of awareness—it doesn't ask us to fix or change what is unfolding but rather be with it as it is. In that space of allowing, compassion begins to grow—first as a gentleness toward ourselves, and then as a tenderness that naturally extends outward.

When we notice our patterns, it's tempting to think, *there I go again* or *why can't I just stop?* Mindfulness asks us to meet those very moments with tenderness.

Sometimes I'll guide a simple practice in class which you can try now, if you'd like. Place your hand on your heart and take one slow, steady breath. Whisper something kind to yourself—something you wish someone had said to you when you were struggling like *It's okay. This is hard. You're doing your best.*

Notice what happens inside. At first, the mind may resist, insisting you don't deserve it or it won't help. That's okay. Keep breathing and repeat it once again to yourself. Compassion doesn't demand warmth or force it to appear; it simply allows the possibility for gentleness to enter. Over time, it becomes a language the body can trust. When kindness replaces judgment, something inside begins to ease a little. When we practice in this way, compassion shifts from an idea into an experience. It becomes something we can touch, breathe, and trust.

This meeting point between awareness and kindness is what researcher Kristin Neff calls self-compassion. She describes it beautifully, identifying three essential elements: mindfulness, kindness, and common humanity. Mindfulness allows us to see our suffering clearly, without denial or exaggeration. Kindness invites us to respond with warmth instead of judgment. And common humanity reminds us that imperfection and pain are part of being human—that we are never alone in them. Together, these qualities form the foundation of self-compassion—the very attitude that softens shame and steadies the heart.

As the language of compassion takes root within us, it shapes how we move through the world. The kindness we practice internally becomes the kindness we extend outward. When we can meet our own pain with gentleness, we naturally begin to meet others with more patience and empathy.

Of course, even with the best intentions, presence isn't always easy. The people we love most can stir up our deepest patterns—the pull to defend, to fix, to control. In those moments, see if you can find the space of awareness first. Take a single, conscious breath before doing or saying anything. Feel your feet on the ground, the air in your lungs, the quiet steadiness waiting beneath the reactivity. Notice the pause between what happens and what you choose to do next. That is the practice—not perfection, but awareness, presence, and choice.

The inner practice isn't a quest for perfect calm or constant kindness. It's the gentle remembering that, in every moment, we have a choice—to pause, to notice, to soften, and to begin again. Each return strengthens the bridge between awareness and compassion, guiding us toward the quiet steadiness within. In time, we realize that awareness and compassion were never destinations at all—they were the path itself, guiding us back to who we have always been. Mindfulness, in the end, is a homecoming—a tender return to ourselves. And with each breath, we find that home has been here all along.

Pause and Reflect

- Think of an ordinary task you do every day—brushing your teeth, walking the dog, making coffee. How might you bring mindful awareness to it today?

- When was the last time you paused before reacting to something or someone? How did that moment of awareness change your experience?

- If you placed a hand over your heart right now, what kind words would you offer yourself in this moment?

- Notice one small way you might carry mindfulness with you into tomorrow—not as something to perfect, but as something to gently remember.

16

Meditations for the Journey

"Peace isn't something we find. It is the quiet strength we return to—again and again—as we meet life as it is." — Jennifer Martin

Mindfulness comes alive through practice—through the ways we remember to pause, breathe, and begin again in the midst of daily life. The more we practice, the more at home we feel within ourselves. What begins as a few moments of stillness starts to ripple through the day, shaping how we meet ourselves, others, and the world around us.

In this chapter, I'll share some simple practices that steady the mind, soften the heart, and remind us that peace is already here, within reach. Each practice is an invitation—a gentle way to return home, one mindful breath at a time.

There is a quiet joy in sharing what has shaped us. When I first began teaching mindfulness, I thought I was simply passing on what had helped me. Over time, I realized that teaching *was* the practice. Each class, each question, each pause invited me to return to what I most needed to remember. I came to see that learning and teaching are part of the same circle. We were all practicing being human—learning to meet our lives as they are. Students often thank me, but more often I want to thank them. The circle teaches us all.

This chapter includes some of the practices that have steadied me most throughout my own journey through mindfulness—the ones that have carried me through uncertainty, softened my striving, and helped me come home to my body and heart. Some are quiet and still; others invite reflection and a deepening of awareness.

As you move through these pages, I invite you to approach each practice as an opportunity rather than an expectation. There's no perfect way to meditate, no single way to be mindful. Let each moment unfold. When the mind wanders, *and it will,* simply begin again. Each return is the practice itself.

Meditation may be simple, but it is not easy. It sounds effortless to sit quietly and notice what is happening inside us—but being truly still with our thoughts and feelings without fixing or distracting ourselves can be difficult. Not only does the mind wander, but the body aches. Time runs short, motivation fades. Some people find that sitting still makes them more anxious at first—and that is completely normal.

We are not trying to stop the mind from wandering; it is the nature of the mind to wander. We are simply noticing the activity of the mind. The practice is to recognize when we have drifted and to gently begin again. There is no failure in that—only an opportunity to start fresh.

Finding the right time to practice can be helpful. For me, it is first thing in the morning, before the day has a chance to hijack my attention. I love beginning this way—it sets the tone for the rest of the day and reminds me to move through it with mindfulness. For others, it might be before bed, after work, or while waiting in the carpool line.

The best time to meditate is the one that actually happens—the one that works for you. You don't have to sit cross-legged on the floor; you can lie down, stand, or walk. The posture doesn't make it a practice—presence does.

Being consistent helps build the muscle of mindfulness—it trains the brain to stay in the present. Just as it takes time to form any new habit, regular practice rewires the mind and body to seek stillness. Over time, meditation begins to feel as natural as brushing your teeth: a quiet, reliable ritual that steadies you for what the day has in store. And when you slip out of your routine, your mind will likely nudge you back—inviting you to return because it misses the peace it has come to know.

Just as consistency is vital for strengthening the muscle of mindfulness, compassion is equally important to the practice. Many of us are already hard on ourselves—measuring, comparing, judging—the last thing we need is to turn meditation into another form of self-criticism. When you notice the mind judging your practice, see if you can meet that thought with kindness. The goal isn't to be a perfect meditator; it is to remember that you are already enough.

You may find one meditation speaks to you more deeply than another, or that different practices support you where you are, depending on the moment. There is no right or wrong. These are not techniques to master, but doorways that lead back to yourself. Each breath, each pause, each act of awareness is an opening—an invitation to remember that peace isn't something we find; it is something we practice.

Exploring Awareness through the Breath

In my classes, I often begin by saying that awareness is the foundation of everything we practice. Before compassion, before acceptance, before letting go—there must first be awareness. It sounds simple, but it is one of the hardest and most transformative things we learn to do: to truly notice what is here, as it is, without trying to change it.

Awareness is at the heart of every practice. Without it, we act out of habit; with it, we have choice. The breath is our simplest way back—always here, always now. Awareness is how we wake up to our lives. We often ping-pong between yesterday and tomorrow—rehashing, regretting, rehearsing, anticipating—and miss the only place anything truly happens: now.

Mindfulness invites us to pause and return—to this breath, this body, this moment that holds our life. Let's begin where mindfulness always begins—with the breath. The simple rhythm of inhaling and exhaling invites us into the present moment.

Breath Practice

Sit or lie comfortably and allow your eyes to soften or close. Feel the support beneath you. Take a moment to check in—how is your body feeling, how fast is your heart beating, how restful or restless is your mind?

Now take a series of three slow, intentional breaths. Inhale deeply through the nose, pause softly at the top, and exhale fully through the mouth. Feel the body settle into this moment. Next, breathe in through the nose and feel the abdomen and chest expand as they fill with air. Feel them contract back towards the spine as you exhale through the mouth. On the third breath, inhale a sense of peace and calm. As you exhale and completely empty the lungs, release stress and tension.

Allow the breath to return to normal without controlling or regulating it in any way. Notice the natural rhythm of your breath—the coolness on the inhale, the softening on the exhale. Let the abdomen and chest rise and fall. When attention drifts, gently acknowledge it and return to the breath.

With each inhale, breathe in tranquility and spaciousness. With each exhale, release any remaining tension or tightness. Let the breath find its own easy rhythm—steady and natural.

When breathing in, notice you are breathing in. When breathing out, notice you are breathing out. Rest here for a few moments, letting each breath renew and soften you.

The Body Scan

When I first began meditating, the body scan was the practice that spoke to me most. Each morning, I'd wake about thirty minutes before our daughters, roll a mat out on the floor, and settle in. I quickly realized how little of my attention lived in my body—I was mostly in my head. But each time I practiced, I began to reconnect, to feel myself as whole again.

Returning attention to the body is healing. It reminds us that even when our body feels unpredictable or unsteady, we can meet it with curiosity and care. Let's explore the body scan—a practice that invites awareness into each part of the body with tenderness and presence.

Body Scan Practice

Lie down or sit comfortably, allowing your breath to flow naturally. Begin with a gentle awareness of your body as a whole—its weight, its contact with the surface beneath you, the steady rhythm of breathing.

When you are ready, bring your attention to your toes. Notice any sensations or simply the presence of this part of your body. Gradually move awareness upward—through the feet, ankles, shins, and calves. With each exhale, let the muscles soften.

Shift attention to the knees, thighs, and hips. Sense any areas of tension or ease, allowing the breath to meet whatever is present.

Bring awareness to the lower back and abdomen. Breathe gently into this space, releasing with each exhale. Move up through the chest, upper back, shoulders, and arms—feeling the breath expand and soften these areas.

Continue through the hands, neck, and face—especially the jaw, eyes, and forehead. Soften the muscles of the face—places where we often hold tension without realizing it. Notice the air at the nostrils, the expression resting on your face.

Finally, sense your entire body from head to toe as one field of awareness—alive, breathing, whole. Rest here, appreciating the body that carries you through your life.

Manifesting Your Intentions

Unlike goals, which focus on outcomes or results, intentions point us in a direction. They are living expressions of what we wish to cultivate for ourselves—qualities like patience, peace, compassion, and joy. You can't fail at an intention. Whatever happens simply becomes part of the practice, gently guiding you back to what matters most.

You might try setting an intention each morning: *Today I move through my day with ease.* Or, *Today I meet myself and others with kindness.* Writing your intention down can help it take root. Speak it aloud. Share it, if you wish. After you have set your intention, let it go. When you release the need to control the outcome, you open to the possibility that life might surprise you.

Intentions can help sustain a regular practice. When I first began meditating, I set an intention each morning: *I am meditating today.* When we tell ourselves, *I am someone who meditates every day,* the mind begins to believe it, and it starts to crave that quiet time. Eventually, meditation becomes less about discipline and more about devotion—a way of honoring your values through your daily choices. You might explore this through the following short intention meditation—an opportunity to pause and connect with the qualities you wish to nurture in yourself.

Intention Meditation

Take a comfortable seat or lie down. Close your eyes and take a few slow, steady breaths. Feel yourself settle—body softening, mind quieting.

Now bring to mind one quality you would like to nurture in yourself today—something that aligns with your heart. Perhaps it's patience, compassion, steadiness, or gratitude. It might be a simple word or phrase: *I choose peace. I am open to joy.*

Let that word or phrase rest gently in your awareness. Say it silently to yourself. Feel its meaning take root in your heart. You might place a hand over your heart as you breathe the words in.

With each inhale, affirm your intention. With each exhale, trust it is already unfolding. Take one more slow breath, and let your intention go—believing it will grow in its own time.

STOP and Pivot: Compassion Begins Within

At the heart of mindfulness lies compassion. Meditation doesn't just steady the mind—it also opens the heart. With practice, we begin to soften our edges and meet ourselves and others with more understanding and less judgment. What we practice grows stronger, and as we strengthen awareness, compassion strengthens alongside it. Compassion is often misunderstood as something we give to others, but in truth, it begins within. When we can meet our own suffering with gentleness—when we stop turning away from what hurts—we create space to extend that same tenderness outward. One of the greatest gifts of mindfulness is realizing that our ability to care for others grows from the same well we draw upon to care for ourselves.

Compassion doesn't mean we won't experience stress, frustration, or pain. Stress is part of being human. Even when we've cultivated awareness and compassion on the cushion, it is easy to lose our footing in the rush of daily life. The emails, the traffic, the unexpected news—all of it can pull us out of presence and back into old habits of tension and reactivity.

If we can meet those moments differently—with brief pauses, awareness, care, and grace, we can respond with intention and kindness rather than be carried away by our own reactivity.

That is why I love teaching the STOP practice. It is a short, powerful way to bring mindfulness into the moments that tend to pull us off balance. You may remember the attorney from my class who drew a small stop sign on his hand with a Sharpie as a reminder to pause before reacting. That is an example of the Stop practice at work.

Sometimes called *the one-minute breathing space,* STOP gives us a way to pause, reset, and respond with greater awareness and care. It helps us step out of automatic pilot mode and back into the present moment. It takes only a few seconds, yet its impact can ripple through an entire day. If we tune into what is happening right now—without expectation— we can find our footing when life feels hurried or tense. You might explore this through the STOP practice— a way to reconnect with our natural resilience and wisdom.

STOP Meditation

Wherever you are, take a moment to pause. Stop moving, doing, thinking. Feel your feet on the ground, the support beneath you. Now take a slow, steady breath in and out. Let the shoulders drop and the breath deepen. Check in with your head, heart, and body. Open your awareness outward—notice your posture, facial expression, the sounds around you. Observe what is happening inside and outside, without judging. Then proceed with what you were doing—with openness, kindness, and no expectation of what should or should not happen next.

Some days, you may only have time for the first two steps—Stop and Take a breath. That is often enough. Remember, one conscious pause can change everything.

Cultivating Loving-Kindness

Once we have learned to meet our own moments of stress with awareness and gentleness, we can offer that same tenderness outward—to the people we love, to those who challenge us, and even to those we may never meet. This is the essence of loving-kindness, or *metta* practice.

Loving-kindness isn't about forcing ourselves to feel a certain way; it's about planting seeds of goodwill in the heart and letting them grow naturally. Because it can be difficult to offer loving kindness to ourselves, we can begin by extending kind wishes to someone we know and care about. Next, we notice what it feels like to offer these same wishes to ourselves. From there, we extend those wishes outward even further like ripples spreading from the center of a lake.

Loving-kindness reminds us that compassion begins within. When we intentionally cultivate goodwill, the heart naturally softens, expanding our capacity for connection and care.

Studies show that practicing loving-kindness can increase empathy, reduce anxiety, and quiet parts of the brain linked to self-criticism. It reminds us that we are all doing our best—that we all long to be happy, healthy, and free from suffering. We all want the same for those we love. Loving-kindness helps us remember that living beings are far more alike than they are different.

To practice loving-kindness is to remember our shared humanity—to recognize we are all connected, each a different expression of the same longing to live, love, and be at peace. This practice restores perspective when the world seems divided, bringing us back to our capacity to care. Let's explore this through a loving-kindness meditation—a practice that awakens our natural capacity for compassion and connection.

Loving-Kindness Meditation

Find a comfortable position and take a few slow breaths. Bring your attention to your heart. When you are ready, picture someone you love and silently offer them these wishes:

May you be happy. May you be healthy. May you be safe. May you be at peace.

Notice what it feels like to wish these things for someone you care about.

Now turn those same wishes toward yourself:

May I be happy. May I be healthy. May I be safe. May I be at peace.

When you feel ready, extend these wishes outward to others in your life—to neighbors, to acquaintances, to people you may know of but don't have a close relationship with.

May you be happy. May you be healthy. May you be safe. May you be at peace

Then, if possible, bring to mind someone with whom you have some sort of difficulty. You don't need to force warm feelings or pretend it's easy. Simply see if you can hold this person in gentle awareness, remembering that, like you, they too wish to be happy and free from suffering. Offering even a small seed of goodwill here can be deeply healing.

May you be happy. May you be healthy. May you be safe. May you be at peace.

Finally, let these wishes ripple outward to include all living beings—humans, animals, plants, and all forms of life on this planet and beyond:

May we all be happy. May we all be healthy. May we all be safe. May we all live with peace and ease.

Rest for a few breaths in this feeling of connection.

Living a Life of Gratitude

When we practice loving-kindness, we begin to notice how care and gratitude are intertwined—how the more we open our hearts to others, the more we recognize the quiet gifts in our own lives. Gratitude doesn't ask us to pretend that everything is perfect. It asks us to notice what is good alongside what is difficult—to hold both joy and sorrow in the same compassionate awareness. It reminds us that even in the midst of pain, there are still moments of beauty: a kind word, a steady breath, the morning light through a window.

In my own practice, gratitude is one of my greatest teachers. During difficult times, it reminds me to focus on what is working, what is nourishing, and what still brings a sense of peace. Mindfulness helps me see that in the midst of challenge; there is always something to be grateful for.

Over time, I have come to see that gratitude isn't something we feel only when life is easy; it is something we choose as a way of living. It shifts our attention from what is missing to what is already here—from what isn't working to what is—and in that shift, peace begins to take root.

Like any mindfulness practice, gratitude deepens through intention and repetition. You might keep a gratitude journal, noting a few small things each day you feel grateful for—the sound of laughter, a moment of rest, a connection shared. Or perhaps, as you lie in bed at night, you silently name three things you are grateful for. Savor each one for a breath or two. This simple act returns you—again and again—to the goodness within and around you. It rewires the mind to seek what's nourishing rather than what is lacking. With practice, we become better at recognizing, savoring, and recalling moments of goodness, and it steadies the heart.

Gratitude can coexist with grief, fatigue, or fear. It doesn't erase those experiences; it simply brings light into them. When we practice gratitude, we recognize that joy is not a distant reward but a quiet presence that grows when we pay attention.

With time, the mind notices what nourishes—a gentle counter to the natural pull towards what is wrong. Let's bring this practice to life now—a quiet way to rest in appreciation for the simple gifts of this moment.

Gratitude Meditation Close your eyes and take a few slow breaths. Bring to mind something you are grateful for—a person, a moment, or something simple like the warmth of sunlight. Let this feeling fill your heart.

Think of another blessing, big or small, perhaps something previously overlooked. With each inhale, welcome gratitude; with each exhale, allow it to radiate outward. Hold this sense of appreciation for a few moments longer, then rest in the quiet fullness it leaves behind.

If you'd like to experience these practices as guided meditations, I've recorded audio versions of the meditations shared in this chapter. They're available on my website which is https://jennifermartinwe llness.com under **When Illness Becomes The Teacher: Meditation Audios**, *and you're warmly welcome to explore them whenever it feels supportive.*

Awareness helps us see. Intention gives us direction. Compassion softens the heart. Loving-kindness expands our capacity to care. And gratitude completes the circle by bringing us home—to the wholeness of this moment, just as it is.

As you conclude this meditation journey, pause. Feel the rise and fall of your breath. Let yourself belong fully to this moment. This is the practice. This is home. May you keep returning to the quiet knowing that everything you need to meet this life already exists within you. Especially on the hard days, remember: you are already enough.

Writing this book became its own meditation—draft by draft, breath by breath—teaching me to return to what is true and to meet it with care.

Thank you for walking beside me, for trusting me to share this space, and for bringing your own presence to these pages.

May the reflections and practices here continue to guide you gently back to your own steadiness. Let them remind you that you matter deeply and that you are never alone. May you keep finding your way home to yourself.

Pause and Reflect

- How has mindfulness shaped the way you meet yourself and your experiences?

- Which practices or moments in this chapter feel like touchstones you can return to in your daily life?

- When you imagine peace—not as perfection, but as presence—what does it look and feel like for you now?

Author's Reflections

Over the years, I tried more than once to write this book. I filled pages, then abandoned them. Each time, the words felt forced, the timing off—as if I were reaching for a story I wasn't ready to hold. Each attempt stalled under the weight of uncertainty—was my story worth telling, was I enough? Again and again, the fear of being misunderstood or dismissed silenced me. Sometimes the words rushed out, raw and searching, only to be deleted in self-doubt. Other times I sat frozen before a blank screen, paralyzed by the whisper: *Who are you to write this?*

Then, after more than two decades of living with MS, years of hard work in therapy, and nearly as long practicing and teaching mindfulness—I was ready. Not because I had everything figured out, but because I trusted that all I had lived through held something of value. I no longer needed the story to be perfect; I just needed it to be authentic.

For the first time, the call to write wasn't fueled by insecurity or fear—it was rooted in trust. Trust that my story mattered. Trust that even the hardest parts—the shame, the uncertainty, the grief—could carry meaning for someone else. Trust that telling the truth of my journey was itself a way of healing. So, I committed. I sat down with a blank page, and this time I kept going. One word, one page, one chapter at a time.

I showed up day after day—not to prove anything, but to honor the voice inside waiting to be heard. What once seemed implausible became possible. Tenderly, the book began to take shape. Even finding an editor was serendipitous. At physical therapy one afternoon, I overheard the assistant talking about a book she had worked on. As she described it, I realized it was the very book sitting on my nightstand. What were the odds? I took it as a sign and asked if I could send her a chapter of my manuscript. From the moment we began, the process gained momentum. Her support, encouragement, and guidance reminded me that we are not meant to walk through life's challenges in isolation. Writing a book is no exception. It was such a gift to have company on the journey.

The original title for my book—the one that sparked my vision years before—evolved as I wrote. Letting go of that title, the one that carried me through years of waiting and false starts, was easier to do than I expected. The title had already done its work, and the story had grown larger than the name that started it all. Releasing it became its own practice of trust. Its purpose fulfilled, my task was simply to follow where the story led.

Trusting life's unfolding often requires loosening our grip on expectations so that something bigger, truer, and more meaningful can emerge. And so, *When Illness Becomes The Teacher* was born. The journey of writing this book put me on an unexpected path of healing. I've witnessed myself growing in confidence, faith, and trust. After a lifetime of hiding the darker parts of myself, bringing them into the light on these pages has changed me. That little girl who tore pages from her locked diary—the nearly sixty-year-old woman who wrote down and ripped up endless pages to keep her secrets hidden—have slowly given way to someone who trusts she is enough.

Postscript: Throwing Away the Key

As I was completing this book, life offered me yet another lesson—an unexpected invitation to live what I had been writing about. Our daughter's recent wedding provided an opportunity to reflect on how deeply mindfulness has reshaped the way I move through the world.

The wedding weekend was a natural extension of this entire journey—a living expression of presence, gratitude, and love. What I remember most isn't how perfect everything was, but how *present* I was through it all. The year of planning unfolded with ease and joy. I was truly able to savor that special time with my daughter. As the wedding drew closer, I felt no urge to manage or shape the day—only a deep trust in letting it unfold as it was. There was so much freedom in that letting go and so much love in the space it created.

The rehearsal dinner was the perfect start to the weekend—a night filled with laughter, stories, and two families coming together in love and friendship. It felt like the start of something sacred. Later that evening, Lindsey wanted to sleep at our home. That simple choice felt like a gift. It was just the four of us—my husband, Lindsey, Carly and me—curled up on the sofa, watching home movies of birthdays and Christmas mornings gone by. The room was filled with laughter and tender moments—a sweetness words can't quite capture.

I grew up watching *It's a Wonderful Life* every Christmas, and that sentiment echoed through me all weekend. I felt it as we watched those old films, as we basked in the warmth of gathering close, and with every hug and burst of laughter. I welled up with gratitude everywhere I looked, spilling over into the smallest details: what a wonderful life it is.

The morning of the wedding dawned softly as I sat at the kitchen table surrounded by Lindsey's closest friends—girls who had once filled our home with laughter and were now women gathered to celebrate her next chapter. The air was light and full of love as we all got ready for the wedding together. I felt deeply content and profoundly grateful, aware of how happy and at peace I was. There was no need to control a thing—only to savor each fleeting, precious moment. In that simple scene, I felt the quiet triumph of being fully present and the freedom to simply be.

The celebration came alive with love—joyful, heartfelt, and perfectly imperfect in all the ways that make life real. What stood out most was the joy in the room: the laughter, the happy tears, and the sight of our daughter and her husband so in love and fully themselves. There was no performing, no worry about what should or should not be—just the freedom to be present and to know that everything was already enough.

The girl who once locked away her words—who tore pages from her diaries and hid her truth—no longer needed to guard her story. Somewhere along the way, I had thrown away the key and learned to love myself into wholeness.

For me, throwing away the key symbolizes giving myself the freedom to be seen, to love without defense, and to let life unfold just as it is.

May this also be your invitation—to throw away your own key, to trust your story, - to live as you are—bravely, tenderly, whole-heartedly.

Acknowledgments

To my husband, Todd, and our children, Carly, Lindsey, and Tanner—thank you for the love that has held me through every chapter of this journey, long before I ever began writing this book. You have been with me through relapses, seasons of growth and change, and the many joys and challenges that have shaped our lives. We have laughed, cried, traveled across oceans, cheered one another on, and shared adventures I will hold close forever.

Thank you for supporting the many hours I spent writing—the long days, late nights, and quiet weekends—never questioning, never rushing, simply offering your steady presence and belief in me. Your love and understanding have been the steady ground beneath every word of this book.

To my parents—thank you for shaping the foundation of who I am and for instilling the values that guide my life. You taught me kindness, perseverance, and faith in possibility. Mom, when I shared that I hoped one day to write a book about living with MS, you encouraged me to follow that dream and even saved the early emails I wrote during my diagnosis. Dad, you showed me the power of mindset and the importance of focusing on what we hope to cultivate. I carry those lessons with deep gratitude.

To family members who have been part of my life from the beginning and those who joined my heart along the way—thank you for your presence and steady support.

To my dear friends—from childhood, from college, and those who came later—thank you for becoming family to me. You have held me in moments of fear and uncertainty, celebrated my joys, and believed in this book even on the days I doubted myself. Your love has been both a soft landing and a source of courage.

To the women in my mindfulness book group—thank you for years of shared learning, reflection, and growth. Your encouragement as I stepped more fully into teaching, your willingness to participate in my series, and the thoughtful conversations that helped shape these practices supported this work in ways that run deep.

To Michelle Hildt and Rachel Thomas at Therapy With Heart, and to Kristine Sinner and Chelsey Pruett at Sinnergy Wellness—thank you for the compassionate spaces you create. Your presence, insight, and support during seasons of growth and healing strengthened my relationships, deepened my self-understanding, and helped me learn to trust myself more fully.

To my editor, Alisa Cooper Wechsler—thank you for your steady guidance, thoughtful edits, and unwavering belief in this work. Your clarity and encouragement helped me bring these pages to life.

To Don McCauley at Free Publicity Group—thank you for your guidance in bringing this book into the world. Your expertise in publishing and marketing has helped transform this manuscript into something tangible and ready to be shared.

To David Cooper—thank you for lending your gifts to help bring the accompanying audio practices to life with warmth and professionalism.

To those who have supported my physical well-being and healthcare over the years—thank you for your skill, patience, and grounded care. Each of you has played a part in helping me navigate this journey with strength and dignity.

I am also deeply grateful for the teachers, authors, practitioners, and guides who supported this work in visible and unseen ways—including Jon Kabat-Zinn and the MBSR community, along with many others whose wisdom lives through these practices. The reflections offered here draw from universal teachings shared across traditions and are offered in the spirit of lived experience and integration.

To the students and clients who have practiced with me—thank you for the privilege of learning alongside you.

Finally—to you, the reader holding this book—thank you for allowing my story to meet yours. I hope these pages remind you that you are not alone, healing is possible, and your inner wisdom has been guiding you all along.

With love and deep gratitude,

Jennifer

Resources for Continued Exploration

Throughout my journey, certain teachers and books have served as steady companions—guiding me through moments of fear, uncertainty, and healing. Some introduced me to mindfulness for the first time, while others deepened my understanding of compassion, stress, and embodied living.

If something in these pages resonates with you, I invite you to begin where you feel called. There is no single right way to build a mindfulness practice—only the next step that feels true for you.

Mindfulness Foundations

Jon Kabat-Zinn – Full Catastrophe Living

Jon Kabat-Zinn – Wherever You Go, There You Are

Jack Kornfield – No Time Like the Present

Jack Kornfield – After the Ecstasy, the Laundry

Sharon Salzberg – *Real Change*

James Baraz – Awakening to Joy

Shauna Shapiro – Good Morning, I Love You

Oren Jay Sofer – Your Heart Was Made for This

Self-Compassion & Emotional Resilience

Kristin Neff – Self-Compassion

Christopher Germer – The Mindful Path to Self-Compassion

Tara Brach – Radical Acceptance

Tara Brach – Radical Compassion

Pema Chödrön – When Things Fall Apart

Thich Nhat Hanh – No Mud, No Lotus

Stress, Science & the Body

Elissa Epel – The Stress Prescription

Amishi Jha – Peak Mind

Gabor Maté – The Myth of Normal

Bessel van der Kolk – The Body Keeps the Score

Rick Hanson – Hardwiring Happiness

Living with Illness, Impermanence & Meaning

Martha Beck – Finding Your Own North Star

Martha Beck – The Way of Integrity

Martha Beck – Beyond Anxiety

Boyd Varty – The Lion Tracker's Guide to Life

Brene Brown – I Thought It Was Just Me

Brene Brown – The Gifts of Imperfection

Brene Brown – Atlas of the Heart

Frank Ostaseski – The Five Invitations

Steven Levine – A Year to Live

Thich Nhat Hanh – No Death, No Fear

Mark Coleman – From Suffering to Peace

Dzigar Kongtrul – Peaceful Heart

Mindfulness Apps

Insight Timer – A free meditation app offering thousands of guided practices, music, and talks from teachers around the world.

IAM Yoga Nidra – Guided Yoga Nidra practices designed to support rest, nervous system regulation, and deep restoration.

IAM Being – A guided Yoga Nidra app offering specially curated meditations rooted in the I AM Yoga Nidra tradition, supporting deep relaxation, stress reduction, and restorative practice.

Guided Meditation Audios

In the final chapter of this book, I share mindfulness practices that have supported me in daily life—moments of pausing, noticing, and returning to myself with kindness. If you'd like to experience these practices as guided meditations, I've created professionally recorded audio versions, available under **When Illness Becomes The Teacher: Meditation Audios** on my website: https://jennifermartinwellness.com.

These recordings are offered as a gentle companion to the book—an invitation to continue the practice in whatever way feels most supportive to you.

About the Author

Jennifer Martin is a certified life coach, mindfulness instructor, writer, and certified Yoga Nidra facilitator. After being diagnosed with Multiple Sclerosis more than twenty years ago, she turned to mindfulness as a path to healing, presence, and self-trust. Over the years, she has guided individuals, groups, and organizations in cultivating greater balance, ease, and resilience through her company, Journey Through Mindfulness, LLC. Her teaching invites others to slow down, listen inward, and reconnect with the calm and clarity available in each moment.

Originally from the East Coast, Jennifer lives in Arizona with her husband and their dog and loves spending time with her two daughters and son-in-law. She continues to write and teach about mindfulness, healing, and the quiet strength found in choosing authenticity.